THE LANGUAGE GAP

The Language Gap provides an accessible review of language gap research, illuminating what we know and what we do not know about the language development of youth from working and lower socioeconomic classes. Written to offer a balanced look at existing literature, this text analyzes how language gap research is portrayed in the media and how debatable research findings have been portrayed as common sense facts. This text additionally analyzes how language gap research has impacted educational policies, and will be the first book-length overview addressing this area of rapidly growing interest.

David Cassels Johnson is Associate Professor of Multilingual Education at the University of Iowa and Visiting Professor of Applied Linguistics at Shanghai International Studies University. He holds a PhD (with distinction) in Educational Linguistics from the University of Pennsylvania. He is the author of *Language Policy* (2013) and co-editor of *Research Methods in Language Policy and Planning: A Practical Guide* (2015, with Francis M. Hult).

Eric J. Johnson is Professor of Bilingual Education at Washington State University. He received his PhD in Sociocultural Anthropology from Arizona State University. His research focuses on ethnographic approaches to immigrant education programs and language policies in public schools. His publications span topics involving bilingual education, immigration, and family engagement.

THE LANGUAGE GAP

Normalizing Deficit Ideologies

David Cassels Johnson and Eric J. Johnson

Routledge
Taylor & Francis Group

NEW YORK AND LONDON

First published 2022
by Routledge
52 Vanderbilt Avenue, New York, NY 10017

and by Routledge
2 Park Square, Milton Park, Abingdon, Oxon OX14 4RN

Routledge is an imprint of the Taylor & Francis Group, an informa business

© 2022 Taylor & Francis

Library of Congress Cataloging-in-Publication Data
Names: Johnson, David Cassels, 1974- author. | Johnson, Eric J., 1974-author.
Title: The language gap : normalizing deficit ideologies / David Cassels Johnson and Eric J. Johnson.
Description: New York, NY : Routledge, 2021. | Includes bibliographical references and index.
Identifiers: LCCN 2020049900 (print) | LCCN 2020049901 (ebook) | ISBN 9781138674004 (hardback) | ISBN 9781138674011 (paperback) | ISBN 9781315561554 (ebook)
Subjects: LCSH: English language–Variation–Research–United States. | English language–Acquisition–Research–United States. | Minority students–United States–Language. | Language policy–United States. | Language and education–United States. | Educational equalization–United States. | Language and culture–United States. | English language–Social aspects–United States. | Sociolinguistics–United States.
Classification: LCC PE2808.8 .J64 2021 (print) | LCC PE2808.8 (ebook) | DDC 427/.973–dc23
LC record available at https://lccn.loc.gov/2020049900
LC ebook record available at https://lccn.loc.gov/2020049901

ISBN: 978-1-138-67400-4 (hbk)
ISBN: 978-1-138-67401-1 (pbk)
ISBN: 978-1-315-56155-4 (ebk)

Typeset in Bembo
by Taylor & Francis Books

CONTENTS

ILLUSTRATIONS

Figures

Tables

1

THE RE-NORMALIZATION OF LANGUAGE DEFICIT IDEOLOGIES

David Cassels Johnson and Eric J. Johnson

In 2017, NASA announced the discovery of seven Earth-sized *exoplanets* outside of our solar system (NASA, 2017). Using the Spitzer Space Telescope, astronomers found the exoplanets orbiting a small star about 40 light years from Earth and named it the Trappist-1 System. Three of these planets, they argue, are within a "habitable zone," which means they are capable of sustaining life. Amazingly, their findings suggest that the orbits are so tight around the small star that the planets take only 1.5–20 days to travel around their "sun." This Trappist-1 ultra-cool dwarf sun is much smaller than ours and, while it should be able to warm the surfaces of the planets, they are not as bright as our world and experience only a salmon-colored daytime light. The astronomers did not actually see the planets; instead, they pointed telescopes at Trappist-1 and measured the amount of starlight blocked as the planets cast their shadows on their sun. Presumably, debate about the details of these findings ensued, and will continue to occur in astronomical circles. However, when these provocative findings were reported by major news outlets such as NBC (Cofield, 2017) and CBS (Lewin, 2017), among others, there was a great deal of interest but no public debate. Why? The astronomers did not actually see the planets through telescopes. No probe had captured photographic evidence. Instead, the researchers used mathematical computations and observations of planetary shadows to argue for the existence of these objects.

Compare this with the announcement from the Oakland Unified School District (OUSD) in 1996 that many of their students spoke a marginalized language variety (African American Language or what they called "Ebonics"), which posed a challenge in classrooms where a school-based variety of Standard American English (SAE) was enforced. Reacting to the low test scores of their Black students, the OUSD argued that African American Language (AAL) speakers faced extra linguistic hurdles because they spoke a language variety that was different from what was utilized in classroom interactions and on standardized tests. So, on December 18, 1996, the OUSD released a resolution that declared "Ebonics" to be the language of its African American students, resulting in widespread media coverage that polarized public opinion. The educators who wrote the resolution were aware of their students' communicative repertoires – they listened to their students every day – and they also had the support of experts: The Linguistic Society of America (LSA) passed its own resolution in 1997 supporting the Oakland School Board's decision (see discussions in Rickford, 1999 and Baugh, 2000; see the full text in Perry & Delpit, 1998, pp.160–161). Furthermore, the ideas in the resolution aligned with decades of linguistic research on dialectal diversity and education: Many Black kids speak a marginalized language variety, which is not reflected, respected, or taught in school. Thus, it was not a new argument nor as scintillating as the idea that there are inhabitable planets perpetually bathed in salmon-colored light 40 light years from Earth.

Yet, the public backlash to the OUSD resolution was loud and scathing: The president of the National Association for the Advancement of Colored People (NAACP), Kweisi Mfume, called the resolution a "cruel joke"; Jesse Jackson declared that it was an "unacceptable surrender bordering on disgrace" (later, Jackson would be more sympathetic); newspaper columnists (e.g., Heilbrunn, 1997) balked at the notion that students' "slang" should be given any respect whatsoever; the secretary of education at the time, Richard Riley, pre-emptively rejected extra funding for the OUSD, even though they had not requested it; racist political cartoons ridiculed the decision (e.g., Huber, 1997). At a congressional hearing about the OUSD Resolution (U.S. Senate, 1997), chaired by Arlen Specter (R-PA), speakers were invited to give statements, including Senator Larry E. Craig, whose credentials included sponsoring English-only legislation; a minister, Reverend Amos C. Brown, who described AAL as a "so-called language"; and a conservative newspaper columnist, Armstrong Williams, who was "deeply troubled" by the resolution and alluded to AAL as "idiom" and "slang" and suggested submersion was the only solution. Upon questioning from Specter about different educational approaches, Williams admitted that he did not really understand Ebonics: "I am trying to understand the Ebonics debate every day" (ibid., p. 66).

Thus, witnesses who had no expertise in language research, and were honest about their ignorance, were still invited to speak as experts. Compare that to a congressional hearing about the development of NASA telescopes (U.S. House of Representatives, 2017) – at which three of the speakers were scientists, one was a director of the Goddard Space Flight Center at NASA, and one was the Director of Acquisition and Sourcing Management for the U.S. Government Accountability Office (presumably to discuss the proposed costs). In other words, all of the speakers were experts in the subject being discussed. What becomes clear is that, in public debate and discourse about language and language education, the voices of the uninformed – even those who admit their ignorance about the evidence and hide behind the claim that it is only their "opinion" – are given prominence in a way that they are not in other disciplines and professions.

Why does the public respond to linguistic findings differently from astronomical findings? Why are people willing to accept the findings from a group of astronomers so much more easily than a society of linguists? There are at least two reasons. First, many of the foundational findings and concepts from language research challenge popular, yet incorrect, beliefs about language and language learning (e.g., Bauer & Trudgill, 1998). Such myths persist because of the second reason: While only a handful of individuals are personally invested in astronomical findings, everyone has a personal relationship with language. As Van Herk (2012) has argued, "Very few people are deeply invested in a particular view of deep space that is challenged by science. But people are invested in their views of [what they consider to be] bad language" (p. 154). Whether or not there are exoplanets that could support biological life does not disrupt the daily lives of non-astronomers. However, linguistic and sociolinguistic research that challenges prescriptive and/or deficit language ideologies can be threatening to those who speak a privileged language variety. Nevertheless, we should listen to the experts because the ramifications for not doing so seriously undermine the economic and educational opportunities for students from minoritized language backgrounds. For most of the history of the United States, educational language policies have systematically marginalized particular languages and their speakers, who are disproportionately students of color. Landmark Supreme Court cases have mitigated the impact of restrictive language policies (e.g., Lau v. Nichols, 1974); nevertheless, race, language, and poverty still continue to shape educational equity for U.S. youth.

Language gap researchers and organizations propose that kids are not successful in school because they do not hear enough (or the right kinds of) words, and the solution is to get their parents to talk more. Putting aside the patronizing suggestion to "teach" parents how to talk to their own kids, we argue educational inequity is more complicated and systemically rooted, and by focusing on language *gaps*, we miss the larger picture of how linguistically and racially minoritized youth experience marginalization both within and outside of school. There is little recognition in the language gap literature of other factors that influence educational inequity – structural racism, poverty, health care, etc. Furthermore, the notion that poor parents are less attentive to their children's (communicative) needs, lack sophisticated communication skills, and are thus less effective parents altogether, aligns neatly with stereotypes that are engendered by neoliberal philosophies that perpetuate a "culture of poverty" paradigm, which blames the poor for educational and economic inequities (Gorski, 2012). By promoting the solution as a panacea for educational problems – i.e., that parents should fill their kids up with words – language gap discourse portrays verbal deficits as *the best* predictor for educational outcomes. Many politicians and educational organizations appropriate these arguments as taken-for-granted facts. Thus, the structure and use of a particular language variety – White middle-class U.S. English – is normalized because of the "prescriptive character of the norm," which positions other language varieties as abnormal (Foucault, 2007, p. 85), and the sociolinguistic and language socialization processes that incorporate them are pathologized (Foucault, 1990).

Normalization of Linguistic Deficits

One foundational theoretical construct in this book is *normalization*. We argue that language gap institutions and policies leverage popular notions about language and language education, which normalizes language deficit ideologies. These language ideologies encompass attitudes, cultural conceptions of language and language variation, shared bodies of commonsense notions about the nature of language (Woolard, 1992). They rely on relationships of power and are part of *habitus*, or socially learned ways of being that provide different amounts of cultural and linguistic capital (Bourdieu, 1977). Linguistic and sociolinguistic hierarchies position minoritized languages and dialects as inferior, while normalizing the dominance of some language varieties and their features as more natural. By codifying certain language forms as the "standard" and promoting them through social institutions (like schools), they become instruments of power that can be wielded and leveraged to reinforce linguistic hierarchies (Bourdieu, 1991). Their hegemonic power is empirically captured in language attitude studies in which speakers consistently denigrate their own minoritized dialect as inferior to other language varieties, which are positioned as "standard" (see review in Cargile et al., 1994).

Language ideologies are durable because of the process of normalization, whereby "a set of simultaneous or subsequent discursive strategies gradually introduce and/or perpetuate in public discourse...patterns of representing social actors, processes, and issues" in ways that privilege the linguistic and sociolinguistic norms of dominant speech communities and therefore leads to the "gradual normalization of key radicalized norms of describing the social, political, economic, [and educational] reality" (Krzyżanowski, 2020, p. 2). Language deficit ideologies are not new; however, we argue that a *re*-normalization of language deficit ideologies is being perpetuated by a new generation of researchers, public intellectuals, and politicians, as well as through foundation and media discourse, which collectively normalize the notion that poor kids experience verbal, and therefore cognitive, deficits. Ideological representations of minoritized families and their language varieties "come to be seen as non-ideological common sense" (Fairclough, 2010, p. 31), which, in the case of the language gap discourse, clearly privileges middle- and upper-class English speakers who do not endure economic and linguistic minoritization. The parents of poor kids are thus scapegoats in the debate, in which non-dominant ideas are silenced through a language gap discourse that normalizes educational inequities for economically disadvantaged children.

While deficit theories about language have persisted for years, Betty Hart and Todd Risley's 1995 publication *Meaningful differences in the everyday experience of young American children* reinvigorated this line of research and popularized the notion of a "word gap." According to Hart and Risley's findings, children from more economically affluent households were exposed to approximately 30 million more words than children who live in poverty. They proposed that this "word gap" between the rich and poor was to blame for substandard cognitive development and a lack of academic achievement in low socioeconomic status communities. This claim has emerged across multiple fields of scholarly research, has been widely embraced by policymakers and educators, and is perpetuated in educational foundation reports and media reports. In fact, a recent Google Scholar search reported over 9,500 citations of the book, which is comparable to Noam Chomsky's *Language and mind*, originally published in 1968, and in its third edition.

Book Roadmap

In this book, we will interrogate how language gap discourse frames families who live in lower socioeconomic status communities and blames them for their own academic struggles. Our goal is for readers to gain a better understanding of: (1) the research that both supports and refutes the language gap, (2) how language gap discourse circulates in the media and in foundational programs and policies, and (3) the educational implications of deficit orientations and ideologies. We have organized this book to provide readers with accessible descriptions of how language gap research is conducted and promoted, while also outlining linguistic, sociolinguistic, and anthropological research that demonstrates the complexity of the human capacity for language.

In Chapter 2, we review foundational concepts, theories, and findings in linguistics, sociolinguistics, and linguistic anthropology that demonstrate the linguistic diversity and sophistication within diverse speech communities. We argue that language gap research mostly ignores this body of work. Chapter 3 offers a review of the theoretical foundations of language deficit ideology, and empirical findings from language gap studies. Chapter 4 examines how language gap discourse is portrayed and perpetuated in the media, and Chapter 5 looks at the institutions and foundations that create and reinforce language gap policies. Finally, Chapter 6 considers the educational implications of language gap discourse, attempts to engage teachers, researchers, and policymakers, and includes a call to action for social justice and educational equity for students and families who speak a minoritized language variety.

References

Bauer, L., & Trudgill, P. (1998). *Language myths*. Penguin Books.

Baugh, J. (2000). *Beyond Ebonics*. Oxford University Press.

Bourdieu, P. (1977). *Outline of a theory of practice*. Cambridge University Press.

Bourdieu, P. (1991). *Language and symbolic power*. Harvard University Press.

Cargile, A. C., Giles, H., Ryan, E. B., & Bradac, J. J. (1994). Language attitudes as a social process: A conceptual model and new directions. *Language and Communication*, 14(3), 211–236.

Cofield, C. (2017). Living on the TRAPPIST-1 planets would be very strange. *NBC News*. https://www.nbcnews.com/mach/space/living-trappist-1-planets-would-be-very-strange-n725206

Fairclough, N. (2010). *Critical discourse analysis: The critical study of language*. Routledge.

Foucault, M. (1990). *The history of sexuality: An introduction: Volume 1*. Vintage Books.

Foucault, M. (2007). *Security, territory, population: Lectures at the Collège de France 1977–1978*. Palgrave.

Gorski, P. C. (2012). Perceiving the problem of poverty and schooling: Deconstructing the class stereotypes that mis-shape education practice and policy. *Equity & Excellence in Education*, 45(2), 302–319.

Hart, B., & Risley, T. (1995). *Meaningful differences in the everyday experience of young American children*. Brookes Publishing.

Heilbrunn, J. (1997). Speech therapy. *New Republic*, January 20.

Huber. J. (1997). On Ebonics. *Politically Correct*, January 8. http://www.conservativecartoons.com/cartoon.php?toon=52

Krzyżanowski, M. (2020). Normalization and the discursive construction of "new" norms and "new" normality: Discourse in the paradoxes of populism and neoliberalism. *Social Semiotics*, 30(4), 431–448.

Lewin, S. (2017). Megatelescope will probe newfound world's atmospheres. *CBS News*, https://www.cbsnews.com/news/megatelescope-will-probe-trappist-1-system-newfound-worlds-atmospheres/

NASA. (2017). NASA telescope revels largest batch of Earth-size, habitable-zone planets around single star. Press release, February 21. https://exoplanets.nasa.gov/news/1419/nasa-telescope-reveals-largest-batch-of-earth-size-habitable-zone-planets-around-single-star/

Perry, T. & Delpit, L. (1998). *The real Ebonics debate: Power, language, and the education of African-American children*. Beacon Press.

Reyes, A. (2020). Spain vs. Catalonia: Normalizing democracy through police intervention. *Social Semiotics*, 30(4), 485–502.

Rickford, J. R. (1999). *African American vernacular English: Features, evolution, educational implications*. Blackwell.

U.S. House of Representatives. (2017). *NASA's next four large telescopes: Hearing before the Subcommittee on Space, Committee on Science, Space, and Technology*. 115th Congress. https://www.govinfo.gov/content/pkg/CHRG-115hhrg27680/pdf/CHRG-115hhrg27680.pdf

U.S. Senate. (1997). *Ebonics: Hearing before a Subcommitte of the Committee on Appropriations*. 105th Congress. https://www.govinfo.gov/content/pkg/CHRG-105shrg39641/pdf/CHRG-105shrg39641.pdf

Van Herk, G. (2012). *What is sociolinguistics?* Wiley-Blackwell.

Woolard, K. (1992). Language ideology: Issues and approaches. *Pragmatics*, 2(3), 235–249.

2

LANGUAGE ACQUISITION AND DIVERSITY

(Socio)linguistic and Anthropological Perspectives

David Cassels Johnson and Eric J. Johnson

If the goal in language gap research is to measure language, we first need to review the concepts, theories, and findings in linguistics, sociolinguistics, and linguistic anthropology to answer the question: What does the research tell us about the nature of language, how humans acquire language, and language diversity in schools? We argue that, with a few exceptions, language gap research ignores this body of research; therefore, the goal in this chapter is to explain some of the fundamental research on language and language acquisition. To do this, we review scholarly work relevant to language gap research, but also include examples from our own families. This literature review informs the critique that follows in Chapter 3.

Perceptions of Correctness: Linguistic Innovation and Language Attitudes

Popular language ideologies position certain language varieties – and particular features within those varieties – as more and less correct or desirable. Labov (1972) refers to these features as sociolinguistic variables, and argues that when a sociolinguistic variable gains widespread attention among a popular audience, it rises to the level of a sociolinguistic stereotype. Such sociolinguistic variables are often a target for prescriptivists who wish to protect the arbitrary rules that govern what is considered the standard form of a language, and a perennial complaint from generation to generation is that the youth are degrading or destroying it. However, while prescriptivists warn against new linguistic features considered to be incorrect or undesirable, language researchers tend to be interested in linguistic innovation and evolution.

What linguists mean by "grammar" is not prescriptive grammatical norms, which are governed by arbitrary rules learned in school, but the innate knowledge speakers have about the rules of language. Grammatical knowledge is creative, subconscious, and ubiquitous among speakers of all languages of the world. Acquiring this grammatical knowledge is not the same thing as learning to tie your shoes, ride a bike, or read a book. It is a fundamentally different process and, unlike these other tasks, it is inevitable – as long as a child is exposed to other humans who talk, they will acquire grammar. Thus, the goal of linguistics is to *describe* how human beings use language, not *prescribe* how they should use language. The latter is the job of lexicographers (dictionary authors), language academies (like Académie Française and the Real Academia Española), and language arts teachers. While linguists do investigate the grammatical rules that make up a prescriptive grammar, the language attitudes they inspire, and the language planning processes intended to preserve them, the primary goal of linguistic research is to understand the human capacity for language, not to control or evaluate it.

As examples of the prescriptivist–descriptivist argument, we present two pronunciation features and two grammatical features, which are considered incorrect or undesirable and are often denigrated in popular discourse: 1) vocal fry – which describes the creaky or gravelly sound at the end of sentences created by vocal fold vibration at low frequencies; 2) high rising terminal (HRT) – popularly referred to as "upspeak" – which describes a rising intonation pattern, typically used for questions, being used for declarative sentences; 3) non-standard "like"; and 4) negative concord.

Vocal Fry

Phonemes can be either voiced or unvoiced. A voiced sound involves a vibration of the vocal folds, and you can feel the difference between a voiced and unvoiced sound by touching your throat while saying /s/ (unvoiced) and then /z/ (voiced). A sound produced with vocal fry – also referred to as glottal fry or glottalization – is a voiced sound, which occurs at a very low register, and is produced when the vocal folds vibrate slowly, creating a creaky low sound. This feature has been described as the "verbal tic of doom" (Chappelow, 2012), "painfully nasal" and "heartbreaking" (Wolf, 2011), and a "debilitating speech disorder afflicting North American women" (Miller, 2015). In reality, vocal fry is not new, not unique to North America, not a nasal phoneme like /n/ or /m/, and is used by both men and women (Irons & Alexander, 2016). To hear examples, one simply can listen to radio DJs (like NPR's Ira Glass), any interview with Noam Chomsky, or a conversation with someone who is tired.

Despite what critics say, vocal fry does both pragmatic and semantic work in utterances. In English and Finnish, for example, vocal fry has been found to be a pragmatic marker that indicates the end of a conversational turn or a syntactic boundary (Ogden, 2001; Wolk et al., 2012). In other languages, vocal fry creates semantic distinctions and is an essential part of the "correct" pronunciation of

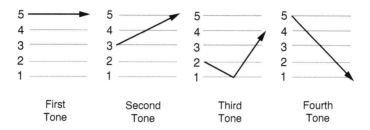

FIGURE 2.1 Tonal variations in Chinese "ma"

tonal languages. For example, Jalapa Mazatec, a Mazatecan language spoken in the Mexican State of Oaxaca, distinguishes between three phonations for vowels – modal (normal), creaky, and breathy (Silverman et al., 1995). As well, Chinese incorporates four distinct tones to distinguish word meaning such that the same word pronounced with different tones has different meanings. In Pinyin, which is the Romanization of Chinese characters, "ma" has four separate meanings based on the four tones: mā (mother), má (hemp), mǎ (horse), mà (scold). As can be seen in Figure 2.1, the third tone involves a dip to a low vocal register, which is often realized as vocal fry by speakers of Chinese when pronouncing words like mǎ. It is actually helpful for English speakers learning Chinese to think about using vocal fry when attempting the third tone.

High Rising Terminal

Like vocal fry, High Rising Terminal (HRT) has been denigrated as an epidemic (Davis, 2010), as contagious as the common cold (Sankin Speech Improvement, 2020), and as a mysterious linguistic infection (BBC, 2014). It is characterized by a rising intonation pattern, which is more common in questions, but used instead for declarative sentences. Popular media refer to this feature as "uptalk" and, like many other denigrated linguistic features, it is often associated with young women. For example, expressing a popular sentiment in a piece for *Psychology Today*, Davis (2010) writes, "It's a nasty habit. It is the very opposite of confidence or assertiveness. It's gotten all out of control" (para. 4).

In an early study of language and gender, Lakoff (1975) identified a question intonation with a high-rising tone at the end of a declarative sentence and argued that it represented powerlessness and weakness. Indeed, this seems to be how it is often portrayed in the media, and research also reveals that it is interpreted as indicating speaker uncertainty (Tomlinson & Tree, 2011). However, empirical studies of its use reveal a multitude of meanings: to show that the speaker was still engaged in their turn, to facilitate others' participation, to assume a position of openness and tolerance, to seek listener verification of understanding, as a politeness strategy, and to indicate a cooperating speaking style (Cheshire, 2003; Gussenhoven, 1984; Levon, 2016; McConnell-Ginet, 1983; McLemore, 1992). HRT is not unique to the U.S.

and has been studied in the UK (Levon, 2016), New Zealand (Britain & Newman, 1992), and Australia, where it is known as "Australian question intonation" (Guy et al., 1986). Furthermore, it is not unique to women (Levon, 2016, Cameron et al., 1988) and has been found to be frequently used by pre-adolescent boys in the U.S., for example (Kortenhoven, 1998).

There are other varieties of English in which HRT is not considered a non-standard feature. For example, Belfast English exhibits frequent rising intonation in declarative sentences, even if in both function and form it is a bit different. In Belfast English, HRT is *consistently* used in declarative utterances but the intonation pattern is slightly different, and might be described as rise-plateau whereby the intonation rises but then plateaus (whereas in HRT it continues to rise). Interestingly, Lowry (2011) finds that women who speak Belfast English are found to use this rising intonation *less*, and a falling intonation (which is more typical of the rest of Britain and the U.S.) more than men.

These distinctions reveal how the same linguistic feature can be denigrated in one context but considered standard in another. Another example is post-vocalic /r/ production (or pronouncing the r after vowels in words like *car* and *park*), which is considered a non-standard feature in the U.S. but is an essential part of Received Pronunciation in the UK (Robinson, 2019). In U.S. English varieties, HRT might be understood as being receptive to communicative needs, while among Belfast speakers, it is just the opposite – a falling intonation is noted as being receptive.

Non-standard Like

Two grammatical features further illuminate the distinction between prescriptive and descriptive grammatical rules: non-standard *like*, and the use of double negatives. Non-standard *like* has been around for decades, made famous in Frank Zappa's song "Valley Girl" released in 1982, and frequently used by the character Shaggy in the Scooby-Doo cartoon. In "Valley Girl," Zappa satirizes the speech of Southern Californians, ridiculing their shallowness: "On Ventura, there she goes, She just bought some bitchen clothes, Tosses her head 'n flips her hair, She got a whole bunch of nothin' in there." One salient feature of Zappa's satire is his impersonation of the Valley girls' speech (voiced in the song by his own daughter, Moon Unit Zappa), especially the non-standard use of the word *like* as in "Encino is like so bitchen." The implication is that the use of non-standard *like* indicates shallowness, especially among young women.

The research confirms that while non-standard *like* enjoys widespread use, it is a stigmatized feature (Blyth et al., 1990; Dailey-O'Cain, 2000). Despite these negative perceptions, however, it is not a meaningless pause filler, but serves pragmatic and semantic functions. For example, it is commonly used as a quotative in the construction "be + like" (Blyth et al., 1990; Romaine & Lange, 1991; Ferrara & Bell, 1995; Tagliamonte & D'Arcy, 2004; Tagliamonte & Hudson, 1999). Quotative *like* can precede both verbatim and constructed dialogue and, unlike the verb "said," it can introduce a thought, pantomime, or gesture. Examples we have collected include the following:

- "And at one point I was *like*, 'Does he want me to come over or what should I do?'"
- "All of a sudden, they were *like* [speaker gestures to his own clothing] 'dressed like this.'"

These uses of like are unique among quotatives, suggesting its usefulness must be one reason for its longevity and ubiquity.

Non-standard *like* is used to provide both looseness and focus to an utterance, phrase, or word. Using *like* to mark what follows as new, important, or somehow salient, is common: e.g.,

- "I've lived in Philadelphia for five years and it's changed a lot...like good change."

Like also provides looseness to either the linguistic form or semantic content of an utterance (Andersson, 1998). It provides distance between a speaker's thought and the linguistic form, and acts as a pragmatic protective shield in case the material following *like* is misrepresented or misunderstood. Brackets are used here to indicate the loosened utterances:

- "There's something in America, like [a factory]...where like [you don't rock the boat]?"

Here, *like* precedes an idiom, thus loosening the form of an utterance that is already distanced from the literality of what is meant. In many cases, *like* acts as a pragmatic or discourse marker and can be deleted without changing the semantic value of the utterances. However, when replacing "about" or "approximately," *like* loosens the semantic content of what follows, as in:

- "I got to bed at like 11:00."

Presumably, the speaker did not get to bed at exactly 11:00 and uses *like* to mean "around" or "approximately."

Negative Concord

Another example is the prescriptive grammatical rule about double negatives, as in:

- She *don't* have *nothing*.

When asked why the rule about double negatives exists, one often gets a response that two negatives equal a positive and therefore it is illogical. Many of us have heard our teachers say exactly this. However, when considering that logic, we might refer to mathematics, wherein two negatives do *not* equal a positive and, instead, two negatives equal another negative. It is not true that adding two negatives equals a positive in mathematics, and neither is it true in language.

Another explanation for why double negatives are illogical relies on the rationale that a second negative item cancels out the first negative item, and thus the sentence "She don't have nothing" should literally mean "She has something." However, consider the following scenario: Suppose you have met a new friend named Yuko and you are telling another friend about meeting Yuko and they ask about Yuko's height: "Is Yuko tall?" they ask. And you respond:

- Yuko is not *not* tall.

Following the logic regarding two negatives cancelling each other out, the meaning of this sentence should be: "Yuko is tall." But, of course, it doesn't mean that at all: the most likely interpretation is that Yuko is neither short nor tall but somewhere in the middle. Yuko is not *not* tall but she is also not *not* short.

Furthermore, the use of double negatives is a common feature in other languages. Consider the following translations of "He don't have nothing."

- Él no tiene nada. (Spanish)
- Il n'a rien. (French)
- El nu are nimic. (Romanian)
- Hy het niks nie. (Afrikaans)
- On nema ništa. (Croatian)

All of these grammatically appropriate sentences use double negatives because these languages use negative concord, the term used to describe a grammatical construction whereby a sentence can contain multiple negatives but is interpreted as being negated only once.

We might also consider the following from Shakespeare:

SALARINO: Why, then you are in love.
ANTONIO: Fie, fie!
SALARINO: **Not** in love **neither**? Then let us say you are sad, Because you are not merry: and 'twere as easy For you to laugh and leap and say you are merry, Because you are not sad.

If these proposed rationales do not make sense, and even Shakespeare used double negatives, why do prescriptive grammatical rules forbid the use of double negatives? The rule goes back to a group of language prescriptivists from the 18th century, the most famous of whom was Robert Lowth. Use of double negatives in English was standard practice at that time, but the argument that two negatives make an affirmative began to gain traction. While he was probably not the first to make the claim (see Tieken-Boon van Ostade, 2010), Lowth popularized this prescriptive grammatical rule with his grammar book *A short introduction to English grammar* first published in 1762 (with a second edition in 1763).

Lowth (1762) issued a series of proclamations about the English language which helped to instantiate new grammatical rules, including: "Two negatives in English destroy one another, or are equivalent to an affirmative" (Lowth, 1762, p. 126). He criticized Shakespeare and Chaucer for utilizing what he called an outdated and ungrammatical form, and argued that Shakespeare's language is an example of "a relique of the ancient style, abounding with negatives, which is now grown wholly obsolete" (p. 139). Lowth was inspired by what he felt was a lack of grammatical accuracy in English and, even amongst the "politest part of our nation" and in "the writings of our most approved authors," it "often offends against every part of Grammar" (p. iii). Propriety was a big concern for Lowth, who desired a tool, long lacking in English, for judging the grammaticality of speech:

> The principle design of a grammar of any language is to teach us to express ourselves with propriety in that language; and to enable us to judge of every phrase and form of construction, whether it be right or not.
>
> *(p. x)*

At that time, there was a desire to distinguish the speech of the working class from that of the aristocracy, and grammar books, which were accessible to only a privileged few, aided this goal.

Linguistic prescriptivism continues to distinguish the speech of people from different socioeconomic backgrounds and, while the rules are often arbitrary, the social repercussions are not. The prescriptivism of Lowth's era has continued to influence language ideologies in schools, which are the main instrument for policing speech and normalizing linguistic hierarchies that privilege White middle-class speech as natural. However, historical evidence reveals how these rules are manufactured. Furthermore, while vocal fry, high rising terminal, and non-standard *like* are used by both men and women, all of them are associated with the speech of women. While language and gender research has moved beyond essentializing linguistic features as statically affixed to men and/or women (Tannen, 1990) – and towards gender as a social construction that is dynamic and performative (Bucholtz, 2014) – in popular culture, particular linguistic features are perceived as prototypically male or female. Sociolinguistic research shows that women are, more often than men, the target of linguistic discrimination (Parker & Borrie, 2018). Labov (2001, pp. 261–293) and Holmes (1997) have argued that

women are at the forefront of linguistic innovation, producing and using innovative forms for variables undergoing change. The edited handbook by Ehrlich et
al. (2014) provides additional examples from sociolinguistic and anthropological
perspectives of how language and gendered norms are reproduced through cultural processes.

These four linguistic features are explored to reveal how attitudes about language
forms engender, and are engendered by, dominant language ideologies, which are
strengthened by sociocultural forces that socialize individuals into such orientations
and acquired identities. While they are popularly stigmatized, analyses of these
features highlight their communicative purpose and sociolinguistic utility.

First Language Acquisition

Pinker (1995, p. 5) argues that "People know how to talk in more or less the sense
that spiders know how to spin webs." It is true that most humans will add vocabulary
words to their linguistic repertoire throughout their lives and, in that sense, they are
always "learning" language. However, the syntax, phonology, and morphology of a
language are acquired early in life and children do not learn the grammar of a language through teaching – they acquire it naturally, and without instruction. Therefore, it is not "learning" in a traditional sense and is more akin to acquiring the ability
to walk or a concept of three-dimensional space. Children are not taught to walk;
they do it as a part of their physical growth and development. While it has been
demonstrated that other (nonhuman) animals also utilize language-like communicative skills (Pinker, 1995), the generative nature of human speech is truly unique.

Theories of First Language Acquisition

A popular explanation for how humans acquire language is that children repeat
what is available in their environment, receive feedback from other language
users like their parents, and respond with new (more correct) forms. This seems
to be the predominant view in language gap research in which environmental
variables and linguistic input are given prominence, which reflects a behavioristic
theory of language learning as proposed by Skinner (1957/2008). B. F. Skinner
characterizes verbal behavior as the same as other behaviors – as a product of stimuli, responses, reinforcement, and habit formation. He argues that verbal
responses are the dependent variable while linguistic input is the independent
variable, and through reinforcement children are taught echoic behavior: "The
echoic repertoire is established in the child through educational reinforcement
because it is useful to parents, teachers, and others" (p. 56). Learning how to talk
continues in school when teachers elicit new responses through new forms of
stimulus control, like "naming objects" (p. 56).

Skinner argues that the "strength" of the verbal behavior relies on the strength
of the stimulus. He has a preference for verbosity (the book is 470 pages) and

celebrates the strong verbal repertoires of, for example, "the scientist who continues to talk shop during a thrilling football game or in a noisy subway and the steamrolling conversationalist who will brook no interruption" (p. 22). (As football fans, we want to emphasize that we do not want any of these shop-talking scientists coming to our house for a game.) As in many language gap studies, Skinner conflates words with language, depicting humans as warehouses of words, and argues that "word counts are often attempts to develop a purely formal analysis of the dependent variable" (p. 27). He also conflates writing with language, which he describes as one type of verbal behavior – learning how to read and write is one part of verbal behavior, which he calls "textual behavior." These depictions of language and language acquisition have been largely discredited by subsequent linguistic research, yet they seem to have found new life in language gap scholarship.

Chomsky's withering critique of Skinner's *Verbal behavior* precipitated a quick demise of behavioristic theories of language acquisition. Chomsky (1959) points out that Skinner lacks empirical justification for his claims, which rely not on analyses of human speech or language acquisition, but on assumptions about the nature of language and analogies to laboratory studies of animal behavior. By using terminology from behavioral psychology (stimulus, response, reinforcement, etc.), Skinner's arguments give the appearance of objectivity but are really just paraphrases for popular vocabulary used to describe language behavior. Chomsky, therefore, characterizes Skinner's claims as arbitrarily based on the experimental literature in which he happens to be interested (behaviorism), yet there is nothing particularly useful about applying behavioral psychology to human language.

Furthermore, it is clear that children do not acquire language through reinforcement or through the "meticulous care on the part of adults who shape their verbal repertoire" (Chomsky, 1959, p. 42). Both children and adults create and understand completely novel utterances, an ability that cannot be explained by environmental stimuli alone. Thus, there must be something else causing the rapidity of language acquisition in children, which Chomsky thought might be an innate capacity for language, although he admits that much more research is needed:

It is futile to inquire into the causation of verbal behavior until much more is known about the specific nature of this behavior; and there is little point in speculating about the process of acquisition without much better understanding of what is acquired.

(p. 55)

(The latter is the focus of Chomsky's [1957] *Syntactic structures*.) Finally, Chomsky notes that all human children exhibit the capacity for language in an astonishingly short period of time and independently of intelligence: "The fact that all normal children acquire essentially comparable grammars of great complexity with remarkable rapidity suggests that human beings are somehow specially designed to do this" (p. 57).

Since Chomsky's critique, first language acquisition research has revealed a number of related problems with Skinner's ideas: 1) humans, children included, are constantly producing completely novel sentences, with utterly unique combinations of words, so it cannot simply be imitation; 2) even when imitating, children vary widely in how much they imitate their parents; 3) parents don't actually correct their children all that often; and, in fact, 4) parents often imitate their kids' errors – providing positive evidence that what the child said was correct (O'Grady, 2005). Furthermore, first language acquisition research has revealed that while some features rely more heavily on environmental input, others – for example, numbers of noun phrases in English, and position of the verb in Korean – do not appear to be related to parental input (Han et al., 2016). As Han et al. (2016) point out, "It is widely acknowledged that what children acquire is not merely a recapitulation of their input" (p. 946).

Since Chomsky first published his ideas, other theories of first language acquisition have emerged, but none outright rejects the position staked out by Chomsky. Emergentism (O'Grady 1999, 2003, 2012) makes the case for a bigger role for the environment. Usage-based theories portray language as not necessarily innate, but the ability to acquire language as innate. Language functions are meaningful, interactive purposes within a social context in which people engage in social interaction (Tomasello, 2000). As Atkinson (2002) describes in his sociocognitive approach to language acquisition, "The social nature of language is not incidental to its existence and ongoing use – it largely if not completely explains them" (p. 526). These perspectives acknowledge the cognitive processes involved in language development as described by Chomsky while also prioritizing the role of the social environment responsible for prompting individuals to use language for the purpose of accomplishing meaningful interactions.

Examples from Child Language Acquisition

Consider the following exchange between a parent and a 4-year-old child (quoted in Cazden, 1972):

1. Child: My teacher holded the baby rabbits and we patted them
2. Adult: Did you say your teacher held the baby rabbits?
3. Child: Yes
4. Adult: What did you say she did?
5. Child: She holded the baby rabbits and we patted them
6. Adult: Did you say she held them tightly?
7. Child: No, she holded them loosely

Most parents have experienced similar conversations with their own kids. Examples of children's language reveal that they do not simply imitate what they hear and, in fact, children often resist corrective feedback from their parents. The exchange above features an overgeneralization by the child, a common and important feature of first language acquisition, whereby the child misapplies a grammatical rule to constructions for which they do not work (here past tense -*ed* instead of the irregular verb "held"). In other words, the child acquires a grammatical rule – add an -ed morpheme to the end of a verb to make it past tense – and then applies this rule to irregular verbs like hold, catch, and run (holded, catched, and runned). They do this even though their parents do not use these words (unless the parents end up imitating the kids, which does indeed happen). In the exchange above the adult attempts to correct the child's error by providing the correct form as a recast in lines 2 and 6 and, yet, the child ignores the corrective feedback in favor of the overgeneralized rule.

Like most parents, we have heard our children say things like:

- I maked a cake last night (Giulia, 4 years)

Even when kids learn the correct past tense form, they will still apply the -ed marker in places where it is incorrect. For example:

- Our feet grewed! (Devi, 3.5 years)
- We broked it! (Devi, 3 years)

There must be something particularly appealing about this rule to make children ignore the input they receive from their environment and continue to overgeneralize paste tense -ed. We have recorded our own children using this particular overgeneralization as late as age 6.5.

Children are always doing inventive things with language, and often parents not only do not correct them, we appropriate their unique linguistic inventions. For example, when (David's daughters) Devi and Mira were two, they were heard fighting in the other room and, soon, one started crying. Devi ran into the kitchen and exclaimed "Daddy, Mira is dizzying me!" This prompted the following command: "Mira, stop dizzying your sister!" *Dizzy* is a common adjective but *dizzying* is a very uncommon verb and rarely used in this way, which makes it likely that she had invented it on her own. By chance she had stumbled upon a real word, but it wasn't because she had heard other individuals using dizzying as a transitive verb: It was because she, like all other kids, was able to do something both remarkable and mundane – invent language based on already internalized linguistic rules about English morphology. Even though noone ever taught her this morphological rule, she knew that she could combine an adjective with the progressive verb ending "-ing" to make a verb. In other words, she had used her linguistic knowledge to make a guess about language. In this case, the guess happened to be correct, in that she correctly used the word, albeit a rare use for it.

Despite what self-appointed language mavens say, *nother* is a word, even if it gets the squiggly red underline in Microsoft Word. At 3.5 years of age, Mira would use *nother* in place of *other*. For example, when asked about the location of some puzzle pieces, she replied, "We don't know where the nother pieces are!" Why this odd bit of language? One explanation might be the following: While "nother" is an uncommon word of English, she had heard the word "another" used a lot. Just like you can separate *a* and *car* in "a car" as two separate morphemes, a child might guess that you can separate *a* and *nother* as in "a nother." In other words, she had incorrectly guessed that the "a" was a separate morpheme in the single morpheme "another" and was the same morpheme as the article *a* in a noun phrase like "a car." Since the nouns that follow *a* in those noun phrases are free morphemes, why shouldn't *nother* be? While this guess resulted in an uncommon usage it reveals the systematicity of child language acquisition.

Child-directed Speech

A popular argument in language gap scholarship is that child-directed speech is necessary to avoid linguistic deficits, even though some research suggests that child-directed speech may not have that much impact on child language acquisition (e.g., Scarborough & Wyckoff, 1986). Child-directed speech is often referred to as motherese or parentese, which describes how caregivers alter their speech when communicating with children. Examples include higher pitch, exaggerated intonation and stress, more restricted vocabulary, and more repetitions. While language gap researchers stress the universality of parentese, other research suggests that it is not universal (Ochs, 1982). While a conversational give-and-take between parent and child might be more common among middle-class families in the U.S., this is not a common speech event everywhere in the world. As Sterponi (2010) points out, middle-class U.S. caregivers tend to emphasize clarifying their children's unintelligible utterances and nonverbal actions. For example, if an infant or young child produces an utterance that is not comprehensible, the caregiver is likely to respond with "Do you mean X?" or "Is X what you are trying to say?" (Sterponi, 2010, p. 239). However, this speech act is not common in other communities like the Inuit (Crago, 1992), the Kaluli (Schieffelin, 1990), or Samoan (Ochs, 1982).

Schieffelin & Ochs (1986) examine how caregivers (do or do not) modify their communicative strategies with young children, and explain that verbal accommodation for children varies cross-culturally along "a continuum running from a highly child-centered to a highly situation-centered communication with children" (p. 174). In highly child-centered (c-c) communication contexts, the caregiver aligns with the perspective of the child. This involves using simplified speech and emphasizing topics that are of interest to the child, which engages the child as an equal conversational partner. On the other end of the continuum, children in highly situation-centered (s-c) communication situations are expected to adapt to the topics, activities, and communicative registers employed by the participants in a given context. Adults in s-c contexts do not use simplified speech and communicate with children according to local norms of interaction. As Zentella (2005) further argues about U.S. parents,

> The c-c [child centered] model is as powerful a part of the dominant norm as Standard English, and its status is such that we tend to evaluate parents favorably if they raise their children in this way and negatively if they do not.
>
> *(p. 19)*

Schieffelin & Ochs' (1986) comparison of interactions between children and care-givers in traditional cultures of Samoa and Papua New Guinea with those in U.S. middle-class (English-speaking) families highlights the differences. For example, the Kaluli in Papau New Guinea assume infants are unable to communicate, so they do not engage them in conversations, nor seek clarification for unintelligible utterances or non-verbal actions. In fact, in both Samoan and Kaluli communities, "there is a dispreference for verbally guessing at the unclear intentions and motivations of others, particularly of children" (p. 173). That said, they find that while "Certain societies appear to lean one way or the other at some particular point in an infant's/ young child's development...other societies such as the Kwara'ae regularly integrate the two orientations throughout early childhood" (p. 174). Further, based on long-itudinal ethnographic research, Watson-Gegeo (1992) observed that Kwara'ae and U.S. middle-class caregiver teaching strategies are similar.

The research on the human capacity for language is robust, rife with debate, and largely ignored by language gap researchers. While some linguists, like Chomsky, tend to emphasize an innate language capacity, others make persuasive arguments for the impact of environmental variables (Clark, 2016). Most would agree that child lan-guage acquisition is a product of both nature and nurture, and the goal is to understand what is dependent on linguistic input and what is not. Nevertheless, barring some kind of neurological or physical impairment that might impede language acquisition, the human capacity for language is universal and first language acquisition is inevitable, even though the type and amount of input children receive varies cross-culturally. Furthermore, the sociocultural contexts in which languages are acquired vary greatly, resulting in different ways of using language and variation in sociolinguistic norms.

Minoritized Varieties and Language Ideologies

A popular and enduring myth is that the speech of people from working-class and lower-income backgrounds lacks the sophistication found in the speech of middle- and upper-class individuals. Linguistic hierarchies are erected around societal attitudes about language, and it is usually predictable which language varieties will be considered most prestigious – just look to how those in positions of power speak. Often, derogatory language attitudes are a reflection of the atti-tudes towards the speakers. For example, throughout U.S. history, language ideologies have fueled language policies meant to restrict particular immigrants from attaining citizenship. Propelled by an insidious nativism, groups like the Know Nothing party and the Immigrant Restriction League (IRL) lobbied for restrictive language policies. The Know Nothing party proposed an amendment to the Massachusetts state constitution which asserted that citizenship and literacy *in English* be a prerequisite for voting and none but native-born Protestants should be eligible for citizenship (Takaki, 2008). This helped lead the way for other states to adopt literacy tests as a requirement for voting. Likewise, the IRL lobbied for a literacy requirement for suffrage and immigration, motivated by antipathy toward Eastern and Southern European nations (e.g., Italy) who, they argued, were "dumping on the United States an alarming number of illiterates, paupers, criminals, and madmen who endangered the American character and American citizenship" (IRL papers, cited in Higham, 1978, p. 103).

The notion that being "American" relies on the ability to speak English is known as a monoglot ideology (Blommaert, 2003), which has been promoted by politicians and judges. For example, in 1921, the Iowa Supreme Court upheld the conviction of a schoolteacher who was teaching German: "The harmful effects of non-American ideas, inculcated through the teaching of foreign languages, might...be avoided by limiting teaching below the eighth grade to the medium of English" (Supreme Court of Iowa, 1921, p. 1060). While the targets of linguistic discrimination have changed throughout history, nativist leveraging of xenophobia and racism to discriminate have remained consistent.

Dialectal variation in the United States is a popular focus of sociolinguistic research, especially those varieties that differ from so-called Standard American English (SAE), including Appalachian English, Hawaiian English, and African American Language (AAL). For decades, researchers have studied these minoritized varieties, with three primary findings salient throughout the body of work: 1) these varieties are not slang, lazy, or improper attempts at English, but, like every other language variety in the world, they are systematic and rule-governed, and differ in predictable ways from SAE; (2) despite these linguistic findings, negative attitudes toward these varieties persist, which leads to stereotyping of their speakers; and (3) with a few exceptions, it is the negative attitudes and stereotypes – not pedagogical or linguistic research on the varieties and their speakers – which have served to create language policy (McGroarty, 1996).

As mentioned in Chapter 1, a landmark language policy around AAL came in 1996 when the Oakland Unified School District (OUSD) became frustrated with the low test scores and grades of its African American students. Along with socioeconomic hurdles, the OUSD felt that many of its students faced linguistic hurdles because they came to school speaking a different language from what was promoted and accepted in Oakland classrooms. So, on December 18, 1996, the OUSD released a resolution declaring that "Ebonics" was the genetically based language of its African American students, resulting in a media frenzy that polarized public opinion (later "genetically" was taken out because of the backlash). Ryan et al. (1982) argue that an important way to assess attitudes toward language varieties is to examine public response – the reaction to OUSD's decision was fervent and revealed how linguistic discrimination is linked to racism and raciolinguistic ideologies (Alim et al., 2016; Flores & Rosa, 2015).

Corson (2000) alludes to Bordieu's educational theories when he argues that students who speak a minoritized language variety are penalized for not speaking a variety that has linguistic capital and status in schools. While many researchers and teachers have responded to these students' pedagogical needs (see Heath, 1983; Rickford & Rickford, 1995), and the OUSD school board made valiant attempts at policy-formation that would accommodate their AAL speaking students, what is still needed is an overarching language policy that attempts to accommodate all AAL speakers throughout the United States, one which recognizes the legitimacy of AAL and the unique challenge – linguistic and sociological – its speakers face.

Perhaps more than any other U.S. language variety, the linguistic features of AAL have been documented (e.g., Labov, 1972; Rickford, 1996). One feature that has received a lot of attention is habitual *be* as in "They be sayin'." The optional deletion of copulas and use of "habitual be" creates a way to express meaning in AAL that is not available in the syntax of SAE.

- He runnin' (He is currently running)
- He be runnin' (He runs regularly. He is a runner).

Sociolinguistic research has illuminated the "logic of nonstandard English" (Labov, 1972, p. 201) across multiple language groups that have been traditionally marginalized and disparaged as inferior. Examples of such work include:

- African American Language (Baugh, 1983; Labov, 1966, 1972; Rickford, 1999; Wolfram & Thomas, 2002),
- Appalachian communities (Wolfram & Christian, 1976),
- Puerto Ricans in New York (Wolfram, 1974; Zentella, 1997),
- Native Americans (Leap, 1993),
- Chicano English speakers (Fought, 2003)

In addition to demonstrating the sophistication of diverse U.S. language varieties, sociolinguistic research on a variety of different ethnic, linguistic, and economic groups has contributed to our understanding of how ideological assumptions about minoritized language varieties distort public perceptions. Framing language varieties as a "deficit" implies that the groups who speak those varieties are somehow culturally inferior. When certain varieties or features are considered inferior, and certain communities are targeted by language gap programs, they may internalize the notion of linguistic inferiority and blame themselves for lacking the knowledge of how to speak appropriately to their children (see video testimony in Thirty Million Word Initiative, 2015). This reveals how language gap discourse perpetuates hegemonic language ideologies that are internalized by those who speak minoritized language varieties.

Linguistic Anthropology

Inspired by anthropology, which focuses on human culture, linguistic anthropology reveals how different cultures socialize children into speech communities. As mentioned, studies of the use of *motherese/parentese* reveals that some mothers talk to their children a great deal while others do not. Nevertheless, all human children develop the ability to communicate effectively and appropriately in their speech communities. Yet, in the language gap research, some socialization practices are portrayed as superior. Linguistic anthropology also provides a backdrop for understanding the power dynamics involved in how communities develop attitudes of superiority and inferiority towards languages and forms of communication between groups. Here, a brief review of findings focuses on *communicative competence* and *language socialization*.

Communicative Competence

As explained by Zentella (2005), "Even before children learn to speak, they begin to learn the rules for becoming a competent member of their society through the language(s) of their caregivers" (p. 15). How children develop their language abilities is determined by the cultural norms of interaction within a given social context. Linguistic features like turn-taking, register, gestures, questioning strategies, and vocabulary vary between groups from different cultural backgrounds. Dell Hymes' (1972) concept of communicative competence explains how social expectations of appropriate language interactions shape the way an individual uses language to participate as a member of that specific community. Hymes' concept helps explain why children acquire specific features of language and it also helps describe why communication breakdowns occur and how communities react when certain individuals do not use expected forms within linguistic interaction.

Communicative competence demonstrates that language patterns considered appropriate in one context won't necessarily be in others. For example, while observing a football game on TV at a local sports bar, it would not be considered out of the ordinary for fans to yell and use profanity if they do not agree with a particular penalty called by a referee. On the other hand, it would be very inappropriate for the same individuals to use the same language with a priest if they do not agree with the sermon. In such cases, social sanctions are usually imposed to ensure individuals know that they are not following linguistic norms within that context. Another example is eye contact. Whereas in some cultures, eye contact demonstrates attentiveness and respect, in other communities, eye contact can indicate defiance and disrespect. When children are raised to understand that eye contact with adults is disrespectful and considered defiant, they are made uncomfortable when teachers expect eye contact to show that they are paying attention. Their reluctance to look at adults in the eyes can cause their teachers to view them as unengaged and lacking interest in school (Philips, 1983).

Schools prioritize English forms associated with a standard, as well as middle class sociolinguistics norms of interaction. When differences are portrayed as a deficit, instead of an asset, proponents of the language gap see them as linguistically inferior to school based English forms. This deficit view reinforces linguistic hierarchies perpetuated by broader language ideologies (described below).

Language Socialization

Cross-cultural research in the field of language socialization illustrates how children acquire "webs of meaning" (Geertz, 1973) and "unconscious patterns of behavior" (Sapir, 1929) through the use of language to become members of a community. Ochs and Schieffelin (2017) explain that

> Language socialization hinges on the potential of embodied communication to engage novices in apprehending and realizing familiar and novel ways of thinking, feeling, and acting with others across the life span. Language socialization presupposes that community members desire and expect children and other novices to display appropriate forms of sociality and competence. Language becomes instrumental in effectuating these ends through symbolic and performative capacities that mediate human experience.
>
> *(p. 1)*

Ochs (1986) emphasizes that language socialization entails "both socialization through language and socialization to use language," such that "children and other novices in society acquire tacit knowledge of principles of social order and systems of belief (ethnotheories) through exposure to and participation in language-mediated interaction" (pp. 2–3). Hence, language use is inextricably linked to an individual's identity and understanding of the world.

Research across multiple cultural contexts demonstrates the varied ways in which children are socialized into cultural ways of being and knowing (Duranti et al., 2014; Schieffelin & Ochs, 1986). This process not only varies between cultural contexts but within them as well. As Ochs and Schieffelin (2014) point out, individuals' "communicative efficacy in particular situations depends upon their grasp of shifting and enduring perspectives that give meaning and order to an array of relationships, institutions, moral worlds, and knowledge domains" (p. 7). While language socialization is especially evident during the initial process of language acquisition, being a culturally competent member of any given community involves adapting to changing contextual forms of meaning across time and place throughout a person's lifetime.

While the process of language socialization is mostly implicit and can be seen as an accumulation of linguistic experiences within cultural contexts, there are instances where caregivers explicitly address their children's communicative competence to emphasize cultural values. In this way, language socialization not only reflects individuals' ability to interact in (socio)linguistically appropriate ways (i.e., their communicative competence), it illustrates an understanding of deeper cultural values and expectations, which are often explicitly taught to children. For example, when children receive something from someone else (e.g., like a present or piece of candy), it is common for U.S. English-speaking parents to explicitly state to their child: "What do you say?" (signaling that the child should reply "Thank you"). This explicit request not only reflects the importance of cultural values involving politeness and gratitude, it also indicates when and how to express them. Sterponi (2010) offers additional examples of parent directives to elicit responses like "I'm sorry" or "I apologize" to emphasize ways of expressing moral awareness, as well as encouraging the use of titles like "Sir/Ma'am" to convey respect.

Although these examples are common in middle-class U.S. communities, they are not universal and cultural values like politeness, gratitude, moral awareness, and respect may be expressed differently depending on the cultural expectations of different communities. Research demonstrates the varied ways in which children are socialized into cultural ways of being and knowing (see Duranti et al., 2014; Schieffelin & Ochs, 1986). As Ochs and Schieffelin (2014) point out, individuals' "communicative efficacy in particular situations depends upon their grasp of shifting and enduring perspectives that give meaning and order to an array of relationships, institutions, moral worlds, and knowledge domains" (p. 7). While language socialization is especially evident during the initial process of language acquisition, being a culturally competent member of any given community involves adapting to changing contextual forms of meaning across time and place throughout a person's lifetime.

Heath's (1983) description of language use in the Piedmont Carolinas highlights how members of different communities within the same region can be socialized to use language in varying ways. The teachers in her ethnographic research reported that the Black students were not responsive to their questions. As one teacher responded, "The simplest questions are the ones they can't answer in the classroom" (Heath, 1983, p. 108). Heath found that the way questions were used in families differed across communities. While White parents used questions to train their children, and frequently asked them display questions (to which the questioner already knows the answer), Black parents asked their children far fewer questions, and rarely used display questions. Thus, while the White kids were accustomed to a type of questioning dominant in classroom lessons, the Black kids were not prepared for the frequency, purposes, and types of school questions. Display questions were prominent in teacher talk, which may reflect dominant educational discourses or the language socialization of the White teachers.

Heath's study also points out how language and literacy practices in the different communities reflect (or not) those prioritized in schools. In the upper-class community, "Maintown" families emphasized structured reading events that involved parent–child interactions involving questions focused on the text. The way that these questions were posed echoed similar patterns expected in school settings (e.g., connections to personal experiences and applications to broader global contexts). Children from Roadville were involved with reading as well, though the questioning focused on components of the story and memorization. Moreover, whereas families in Trackton had reading materials, they were most commonly linked to church contexts and not commonly read at home, and rarely on an individual basis.

When language socialization research is applied to a school setting, it is easy to see why proponents of the language gap are quick to assign blame to the communication patterns of the home. Children from privileged economic backgrounds generally grow up in households with caregivers who speak in a similar fashion as teachers, and are exposed to books that are similar to those used in schools. When these children get to school, they have already been socialized into ways of interacting, understanding, and engaging with texts, which are reflected and privileged in school discourse. The language gap argument implies that children from low-income backgrounds are at a developmental disadvantage based on the language practices within their homes and, thus, must be supported by training their parents to communicate differently. In other words, as Zentella (2005) points out, "the more the child has a caregiver who acts like a teacher, the more the child is considered educable" (p. 24). So taken-for-granted is this view that it is easy to overlook how language patterns used in school represent only a limited range of (socio)linguistic possibilities for interacting in the world.

Obligating parents to change their language practices directly affects the ways that children acquire cultural knowledge and values that are meaningful to their family. Zentella encourages us to avoid the pitfall of "the privileging of literate behaviors and the greater respect given to parents who follow a teacher model of parenting" (p. 24), which can preclude teachers from accessing the linguistic and cultural assets students bring with them to the classroom. Consistently directing parents to speak more words with their children and interact differently to enhance the "quality" of their language patterns tacitly communicates the message that their language, identity, and cultural norms are inferior to those promoted in schools. The process of shaping social perspectives towards language(s) and language forms has immense social implications, and is best described through a language ideologies framework.

The Language of Schooling

So, what is it about academic contexts and the language patterns used in schools that tends to pose challenges for students from diverse backgrounds? Can academic struggles even be boiled down to issues of language? Tending to these important questions will help illustrate the misguided nature of casting blame on parents' language use for their children's academic struggles.

Prescriptivism and Academic Language

Building on the notion of linguistic prescriptivism mentioned above, we now focus on how prescriptive orientations manifest within schools and classroom settings. Crystal's (1986) definition of prescriptivism is particularly germane to our discussion:

> In its most general sense, prescriptivism is the view that one variety of language has an inherently higher value than others, and that this ought to be imposed on the whole of the speech community...Adherents to this variety are said to speak or write 'correctly'; deviation from it are said to be 'incorrect'.
>
> *(p. 2)*

Schools are crucial to the perpetuation of prescriptive views of English. As Milroy & Milroy (2012) explain, "Prescription depends on an ideology (or set of beliefs) concerning language which requires that in language use, as in other matters, things shall be done in the 'right' way" (p. 1). This orientation of "correctness" is policed by schools through formal assessments and between teachers and students. One goal of schooling is to teach the orthographic, phonological, and syntactic conventions that reflect what is perceived as Standard American English (SAE), and to guide students in how to use formal speaking registers. The social and economic benefits of such an education are clear. However, an emphasis on prescriptive norms need not subjugate and denigrate, and can be coupled with, diverse cultural and sociolinguistic practices (Paris & Alim, 2017). Many teachers do this already – especially in bilingual education classrooms – by engaging the diverse language repertoires of students to simultaneously facilitate their academic progress while developing "critical language awareness" (Alim, 2005).

Even though prescriptive forms are framed as linguistically superior, much of their strength relies on arbitrary rules that are promoted by groups in dominant political and economic positions of power to sustain their own language patterns (Lippi-Green, 2012). Most people recognize the notion of "academic language" as a common way to refer to the language patterns that are used in school – though there is little consensus on an overall coherent definition (Faltis, 2013). Current descriptions have been informed by a variety of different scholarly disciplines spanning education, anthropology, communication, sociology, psychology, and many others (Gottlieb & Ernst-Slavit, 2014; Valdés, 2004). A common point of contention is the distinction between "social" and "academic" language.

Cummins (1984) popularized this distinction by promoting his notion of children who could speak in social situations (e.g., on the playground) as having *basic interpersonal communication skills* (BICS), but students who struggled with language demands in school were lacking *cognitive academic language proficiency* (CALP).

While this influential proposal has prompted educators to focus on enhancing language support for linguistically diverse students, it contributed to a deficit ideology by portraying children who struggle in school as only having "basic" language skills and lacking "cognitive" skills (Faltis, 2013; MacSwan & Rolstad, 2003). A basic premise of the social/academic language dichotomy rests on the notion that whereas social language forms are "contextualized" and based on face-to-face interactions, "decontextualized" language forms are conceptually abstract and rely on explicit uses of words and phrases for descriptive purposes, with little assumed about the receiver of the communication. Gee (2000) argues that the dichotomy is illogical since all uses of language, either through oracy or literacy, are contextualized and, within any given linguistic interaction, students are engaged in language events that have been constructed through broader sociocultural forces. As Gee (2014) points out, this theory also

> fails to tell us why schools do not or cannot teach disadvantaged children decontextualized language (and the variety of different practices in which it is recruited) and why it does not or cannot catch them up with their more advantaged peers, despite the home and community support such children have.
>
> *(p. 11)*

The verbal interactions and literacy activities used for all instructional purposes are all contextualized within a social event: *schooling*. The degree to which students are able to conceptually access the content within these contexts is determined by factors that span immediate uses of language to policy processes unseen by students and teachers. Adding another layer of complexity to these examples is the fact that schooling contexts span multiple content areas (e.g., math, science, social studies, etc.), all of which have varying language and social interactional demands (Gottlieb & Ernst-Slavit, 2014). All of these factors, among countless others, impact the degree of meaningfulness that academic content has for students. Thus, as Gee (2014) notes, "In the end, many children fail in school, because schools create no meaningful contexts…The problem of school failure is not that certain children fail to master decontextualized language. It is that, for some children, language at school is decontextualized" (p. 22).

This analysis of prescriptivism and academic language is intended to shed light on how the language gap (mis)represents academic challenges as rooted in linguistic deficiencies of families from low income backgrounds. Connecting poverty to language practices that derail students' scholastic progress is an oversimplification of both language and education, not to mention poverty. Moreover, conceptual discontinuities in classrooms occur when academic subject matter is not made meaningful and/or the content is not relevant to students. When teachers cannot tap into students' language patterns to enhance the way concepts are conveyed in academic contexts, the students are obstructed from accessing the concept. Beyond teachers impeding access to meaning through their language use, when students' linguistic identities are called into question (as inferior), they are affectively distanced from the learning environment which, in turn, derails their educational "investment" (Johnson & Johnson, 2016; Norton, 1995).

Cultural Diversity and Learning

Absent from language gap discourse are analyses of how broader social contexts shape the experiences of linguistically diverse students. As Faltis (2013) contends,

> It is not farfetched to consider why bilingual children and youth may not want to affiliate with the academic communities schools value, when in the broader social contexts, they and their families are afforded limited access to power based on pervasive views about their language abilities, social class, and ethnic backgrounds.
>
> *(p. 21)*

The language gap becomes a scapegoat for all social and academic woes, while more fundamental issues involving inter-group perceptions and relationships are ignored. Not only does the language gap blame parents for their children's academic challenges, it reinforces stereotypes that linguistically diverse communities are ill-equipped to raise their children. The proliferation of parental language remediation programs and increasing scholarship on the language gap has produced a billow in media coverage (Johnson et al., 2017) and recasts historically rooted inequities as grounded in language disparities.

Instead of ignoring the verbal repertoires of students, drawing on students' background experiences and knowledge can enhance academic experiences (Johnson & Johnson, 2016). Research is abundant with the examples of, and need for, building upon students' *funds of knowledge*. "Funds of knowledge" refers to an individual's historically accumulated set of abilities, strategies, or bodies of knowledge (González et al., 2005; Vélez-Ibáñez & Greenberg, 1992). These "funds" can be recognized by observing "the wider set of activities requiring specific strategic bodies of essential information that households need to maintain their well-being" (Vélez-Ibáñez & Greenberg, 1992, p. 314). Funds of knowledge encompass both academic and personal background knowledge, accumulated life experiences, skills used to navigate everyday social contexts, and world view(s) structured by broader historically situated sociocultural forces.

Instead of looking at language differences as pathologies to cure, applying a funds of knowledge approach to understanding students' overall sets of linguistic and cultural experiences can help teachers draw on these skills in classrooms to engage their students during academic activities. For example, in their research on engaging students and families outside of school contexts, Kyle et al. (2005) found that a "deeper understanding of the funds of knowledge held by families became a source [that] teachers drew upon in the immediacy of teaching, making subtle adjustments and connections to help children feel known and a part of the learning taking place" (p. 44). This orientation moves away from seeing "word/language gaps" to recognizing what educational anthropologist Marjorie Faulstich Orellana (2017) describes as "word wealth" – i.e., the abundance of linguistic knowledge that linguistically diverse families possess.

The converse of deficit perspectives like the language gap involves pointing out the deficiencies that schools have in terms of understanding: 1) how to recognize and value diverse cultural and linguistic patterns as assets, and 2) how to integrate those cultural and linguistic strengths into the classroom. This extends to teacher preparation programs and professional development initiatives that fail to equip educators with the tools to reframe their approach to working with culturally and linguistically diverse students and families. As Faltis (2013) argues,

> unless we also seriously address the cultural baggage of standard language, pre-scriptivism, market value references, and deficit-oriented conceptualizations of social language and bilingualism, efforts to prepare teachers and students to understand and become proficient in academic language are unlikely to yield significant changes in the educational and social achievement of bilingual children and youth.
>
> *(pp. 21–22)*

It is from this orientation towards language, poverty, and education that we analyze language gap discourse in hopes of providing scholars, practitioners, and community members a critical framework for confronting the deficit ideologies that uphold language gap programs and rethinking approaches for supporting culturally and linguistically diverse students and families.

Conclusion: Language Ideologies and Deficit Discourses

The process of shaping social perspectives towards language(s) and language forms has immense social implications and can be viewed through a language ideologies framework (Kroskrity, 2006; Woolard & Scheiffelin, 1994). Language ideologies encompass attitudes, cultural conceptions of language and language variation, and shared bodies of commonsense notions about the nature of language, and position particular features/varieties as more natural (Woolard, 1992). Ideologies are not static, but emerge in a dynamic process involving the production of meanings and ideas such that beliefs are constantly (re)shaped through social interactions. This view of ideology underscores the fluid and interactional nature of the forces that channel social relationships and practices such that the practices of certain groups are seen as superior (i.e., normal, good, correct) over others (Woolard, 1998).

Linguistic and sociolinguistic hierarchies position minoritized languages and dialects as inferior and *normalize* the dominance of some language varieties. Language ideologies are durable because of the process of normalization, whereby discourses that perpetuate hegemonic linguistic and sociolinguistic hierarchies that privilege White middle- and upper-class language features are portrayed as natural, instead of as constructions of power relationships (Krzyżanowski, 2020). In seeking to explain educational inequity for students from low-income backgrounds, language gap research relies on, and perpetuates, dominant language ideologies that position linguistic and sociolinguistic features of middle- and upper-class communities as superior. Milroy (2001) describes contexts in which members of a given society share a hierarchical view towards dialectal variation as a "standard language culture." According to Milroy, "standardization works by promoting invariance or uniformity in a language structure" (p. 531).

Language deficit ideologies are not new, but language gap research has legitimized and breathed new life into a re-normalization of language deficits. Sometimes this is explicitly expressed; for example, Hoff (2013) argues that "[b]y the pragmatic criterion of usefulness for academic success, the different skills of lower SES [socioeconomic status] children constitute a deficit" (p. 7). Absent in Hoff's evaluation of low-income children's language abilities is a description of other social, linguistic, and pedagogical factors that negatively influence the academic progress of low-income and minoritized students (a consistent omission in language gap research). Language gap researchers thus give educators a ready-made excuse to denigrate their students' language. For example, a teacher in Arizona who works with bilingual students (Spanish/English) in a low-income school district expressed his perspective of what counts as good versus bad language skills: "I try to tell these kids that they're extremely lucky that they're bilingual, [but] I tell these guys you can know street Spanish, but you're not going to get a decent job" (Johnson, 2011, p. 15).

To this teacher, although being bilingual was seen as valuable, the variety of Spanish spoken by his students was inferior. Furthermore, even though this particular teacher was not bilingual himself, and could not point out any specific linguistic features that distinguished his students' dialect of Spanish as compared to an imagined "superior" dialect of Spanish, he was confident that "street Spanish" was inferior and carried no economic advantage.

Commonsense notions of linguistic superiority – as reflected in the language gap – that promote popular, if incorrect, beliefs about the human capacity for language are inextricably linked to larger "regimes of language" (Kroskrity, 2000) that contribute to social hierarchies between different linguistic, cultural, and economic groups. In other words, how the linguistic patterns of low-income families are portrayed by the language gap contributes to the reproduction of broader societal beliefs about the linguistic competency and intellectual capacity of individuals from economically disadvantaged communities. This does little to challenge the real educational inequities experienced by students who speak minoritized language varieties and/or come from low-income backgrounds.

References

Alim, H. S. (2005). Critical language awareness in the United States: Revisiting issues and revising pedagogies in a resegregated society. *Educational Researcher*, 34(7), 24–31.

Alim, H. S., Rickford, J. R., & Ball, A. F. (Eds.) (2016). *Raciolinguistics: How language shapes our ideas about race.* Oxford University Press.

Andersson, L. G. (1998). *Some languages are harder than others.* In L. Bauer & P. Trudgill (Eds.), *Language myths* (pp. 50–57). Penguin Books.

Atkinson, D. (2002). Toward a sociocognitive approach to second language acquisition. *Modern Language Journal*, 85(4), 525–545.

BBC. (2014). The unstoppable march of the upward inflection. *BBC News*, August 11. https://www.bbc.com/news/magazine-28708526

Baugh, J. (1983). *Black street speech: Its history, structure, and survival.* University of Texas Press.

Blommaert, J. (2003). Commentary: A sociolinguistics of globalization. *Journal of Sociolinguistics*, 7(4), 607–623.

Blyth, C., Recktenwald, S., & Wang, J. (1990). I'm like, 'Say what?!': A new quotative in American oral narrative. *American Speech*, 65(3), 215–227.

Britain, D., & Newman, J. (1992). High rising terminals in New Zealand English. *Journal of the International Phonetic Association*, 22(1/2), 1–11.

Bucholtz, M. (2014). The feminist foundations of language, gender, and sexuality research. In S. Ehrlich, M. Meyerhoff & J. Holmes (Eds.), *The handbook of language, gender, and sexuality* (pp. 23–47). John Wiley & Sons.

Cameron, D., McAlinden, F., & O'Leary, K. (1988). Lakoff in context: The social and linguistic functions of tag questions. In J. Coates & D. Cameron (Eds.), *Women's language: Critical approaches* (pp. 74–93). Routledge.

Cazden, C. (1972). *Child language and education.* Holt, Rinehart, & Winston.

Chappelow, C. (2012). The verbal tic of doom: Why the "vocal fry" is killing your job search. *Fast Company*, April 19. https://www.fastcompany.com/1834461/verbal-tic-doom-why-the-vocal-fry-killing-your-job-search

Cheshire, J. (2003). Social dimensions of syntactic variation: The case of when clauses. In D. Britain & J. Cheshire (Eds.), *Social dialectology: In honour of Peter Trudgill* (pp. 245–261). Benjamins.

Chomsky, N. (1957). *Syntactic structures.* Mouton & Co.

Chomsky, N. (1959). Review of Skinner's 'verbal behavior'. *Language*, 35(1), 26–58.

Clark, E. V.(2016). *First language acquisition.* Cambridge University Press.

Corson, D. (2000). *Language diversity and education.* Routledge.

Crago, M. B. (1992). Communicative interaction and second language acquisition: An Inuit example. *TESOL Quarterly*, 26(3), 487–505.

Crystal, D. (1986). The prescriptive tradition. In D. Crystal (Ed.), *The Cambridge encyclopedia of language* (pp. 2–5). Cambridge University Press.

Cummins, J. (1984) *Bilingualism and special education: Issues in assessment and pedagogy.* Multilingual Matters.

Dailey-O'Cain, J. (2000). The sociolinguistic distribution of and attitudes toward focuser like and quotative like. *Journal of Sociolinguistics,* 4(1), 60–80.

Davis, H. (2010). The uptalk epidemic. *Psychology Today,* October 6. https://www.psychologytoday.com/us/blog/caveman-logic/201010/the-uptalk-epidemic

Druanti, A., Ochs, E., & Schieffelin, B. B. (Eds.). (2014). *The handbook of language socialization.* Wiley Blackwell.

Ehrlich, S., Meyerhoff, M., & Holmes, J. (Eds.). (2014). *The handbook of language, gender, and sexuality.* Wiley Blackwell.

Faltis, C. (2013). Demystifying and questioning the power of academic language. In M. B. Arias & C. Faltis (Eds.), *Academic language in second language learning* (pp. 3–26). Information Age Publishing.

Ferrara, K., & Bell, B. (1995). Sociolinguistic variation and discourse function of constructed dialogue introducers: The case of be + like. *American Speech,* 70(3), 265–290.

Flores, N., & Rosa, J. (2015). Undoing appropriateness: Raciolinguistic ideologies and language diversity in education. *Harvard Educational Review,* 85(2), 149–171.

Fought, C. (2003). *Chicano English in context.* Palgrave Macmillan.

Gee, J. (2000). New people in new worlds: Networks, the new capitalism and schools. In C. Cope & M. Kalantzis (Eds.), *Multiliteracies: Literacy learning and the design of social futures* (pp. 41–66). Routledge.

Gee, J. (2014). Decontextualized language: A problem, not a solution. *International Multilingual Research Journal,* 8(1), 9–23.

Geertz, C. (1973). *The interpretation of cultures.* Basic Books.

González, N., Moll, L. C., & Amanti, C. (Eds.). (2005). *Funds of knowledge: Theorizing practices in households, communities, and classrooms.* Routledge.

Gottlieb, M., & Ernst-Slavit, G. (2014). *Academic language in diverse classrooms.* Corwin.

Gussenhoven, C. (1984). A semantic analysis of the nuclear tones of English. In C. Gussenhoven (Ed.), *On the grammar and semantics of sentence accents* (pp. 193–265). Foris Publications.

Guy, G., Horvath, B. M., Vonwiller, J., & Rogers, I. (1986). An intonational change in progress in Australian English. *Language in Society,* 15(1), 23–51.

Han, C. H., Musolino, J., & Lidz, J. (2016). Endogenous sources of variation in language acquisition. *Proceedings of the National Academy of Sciences,* 113(4), 942–947.

Heath, S. B. (1983). *Ways with words: Language, life and work in communities and classrooms.* Cambridge University Press.

Higham, J. (1978). *Strangers in the land: Patterns of American nativitism, 1860–1925.* Rutgers University Press.

Hoff, E. (2013). Interpreting the early language trajectories of children from low-SES and language minority homes: implications for closing achievement gaps. *Developmental Psychology,* 49(1), 4–14.

Holmes, J. (1997). Women, language and identity. *Journal of Sociolinguistics,* 1(2), 195–223.

Hymes, D. (1972). On communicative competence. In J. B. Pride & J. Holmes (Eds.), *Sociolinguistics: Selected readings.* (pp. 269–293). Penguin.

Irons, S. T., & Alexander, J. E. (2016). Vocal fry in realistic speech: Acoustic characteristics and perceptions of vocal fry in spontaneously produced and read speech. *Journal of the Acoustical Society of America,* 140(4), 3397.

Johnson, E. J. (2011). (Re)producing linguistic hierarchies in the United States: Language ideologies of function and form in public schools. *International Journal of Linguistics,* 3(1), E12.

Johnson, E. J., Avineri, N., & Johnson, D. C. (2017). Exposing gaps in/between discourses of linguistic deficits. *International Multilingual Research Journal*, 11(1), 5–22.

Johnson, E. J., & Johnson, A. B. (2016). Enhancing academic investment through home-school connections and building on ELL students' scholastic funds of knowledge. *Journal of Language & Literacy Education*, 12(1), 104–121.

Kortenhoven, A. (1998). Rising intonation in children's narratives. Unpublished manuscript.

Kroskrity, P. V. (2000). *Regimes of language: Ideologies, polities, and identities*. School of American Research Press.

Kroskrity, P. V. (2006). Language ideologies. In A. Duranti (Ed.), *A companion to linguistic anthropology* (pp. 496–517). Blackwell.

Krzyżanowski, M. (2020). Normalization and the discursive construction of "new" norms and "new" normality: Discourse in the paradoxes of populism and neoliberalism. *Social Semiotics*, doi:10.1080/10350330.2020.1766193.

Kyle, D. W., McIntyre, E., Miller, K. B., & Moore, G. H. (2005). Family connections: A basis for teacher reflection and instructional improvement. *School Community Journal*, 15(1), 15–28.

Labov, W. (1966). *The social stratification of English in New York City*. Cambridge University Press.

Labov, W. (1972). *Language in the inner city: Studies in the black English vernacular*. University of Pennsylvania Press.

Labov, W. (2001). *Principles of linguistic change, Vol. 2: Social factors*. Blackwell.

Lakoff, R. (1975). *Language and woman's place: Text and commentaries*. Harper & Row.

Leap, W. (1993). *American Indian English*. University of Utah Press.

Levon. E. (2016). Gender, interaction and intonational variation: The discourse functions of high rising terminals in London. *Journal of Sociolinguistics*, 20(2), 133–163.

Lippi-Green, R. (2012). *English with an accent: Language, ideology, and discrimination in the United States*. Routledge.

Lowry, O. (2011). Belfast intonation and speaker gender. *Journal of English Linguistics*, 39(3), 209–232.

Lowth, R. (1762). *A short introduction to English grammar with critical notes*. J. Hughs.

MacSwan, J., & Rolstad, K. (2003). Linguistic diversity, schooling, and social class: Rethinking our conception of language proficiency in language minority education. In C. B. Paulston & R. Tucker (Eds.), *Sociolinguistics: The essential readings* (pp. 329–340). Blackwell.

McConnell-Ginet. S. (1983). Intonation in a man's world. In B. Thorne, C. Kramarae & N. Henly (Eds.), *Language, gender, and society* (pp. 69–88). Newbury House.

McGroarty, M. (1996). Language attitudes, motivation and standards. In S. McKay & N. Hornberger (Eds.), *Sociolinguistics and language teaching* (pp. 3–46). Cambridge University Press.

McLemore, C. (1992). The interpretation of LH in English. In C. McLemore (Ed.), *Texas linguistic forum 32* (pp. 175–196). University of Texas Department of Linguistics and the Center for Cognitive Science.

Miller, L. (2015). The debilitating speaking disorder afflicting North American women. *ABC Correspondents Report*, February 1. http://www.abc.net.au/correspondents/content/2015/s4171748.htm

Milroy, J. (2001). Language ideologies and the consequences of standardization. *Journal of Sociolinguistics*, 5(4), 530–555.

Milroy, J., & Milroy, L. (2012). *Authority in language: Investigating standard English*. Routledge.

Norton, B. (1995). Social identity, investment, and language learning. *TESOL Quarterly*, 29(1), 9–31.

Ochs, E. (1982). Talking to children in Western Samoan. *Language in Society*, 11(1), 77–104.

Ochs, E. (1986). Introduction. In B. B. Schieffelin & Elinor Ochs (Eds.), *Language socialization across cultures* (pp. 1–13). Cambridge University Press.

Ochs, E., & Schieffelin, B. (2014). The theory of language socialization. In A. Druanti, E. Ochs & B. B. Schieffelin (Eds.), *The handbook of language socialization* (pp. 1–22). Wiley Blackwell

Ochs, E., & Schieffelin, B. (2017). Language socialization: An historical overview. In P. A. Duff & S. May (Eds.), *Encyclopedia of language and education, language socialization* (pp. 1–14). Springer International.

Ogden, R. (2001). Turn-holding, turn-yielding, and laryngeal activity in Finnish talk-in interaction. *Journal of the International Phonetics Association*, 31, 139–152.

O'Grady, W. (1999). Toward a new nativism. *Studies in Second Language Acquisition*, 21, 621–633.

O'Grady, W. (2003). The radical middle: Nativism without universal grammar. In C. Doughty & M. Long (Eds.), *The handbook of second language acquisition* (pp. 42–103). Blackwell Publishing.

O'Grady, W. (2005). *How children learn language*. Cambridge University Press.

O'Grady, W. (2012). Language acquisition without an acquisition device. *Language Teaching*, 45, 116–130.

Orellana, M. F. (2017). A different kind of word gap. *Huffington Post*, May 19. https://www.huffpost.com/entry/a-different-kind-of-word_b_10030876

Parker, M. A., & Borrie, S. A. (2018). Judgements of intelligibility and likeability of young adult female speakers of American English: The influence of vocal fry and the surrounding acoustic-prosodic context. *Journal of Voice*, 32(5), 538–545.

Paris, D., & Alim, S. H. (Eds.). (2017). *Culturally sustaining pedagogies: Teaching and learning for justice in a changing world*. Teachers College Press.

Philips, S. U. (1983). *The invisible culture: Communication in classroom and community on the Warm Springs Reservation*. Waveland Press.

Pinker, S. (1994). *The language instinct: How the mind creates language*. William Morrow and Company.

Pinker, S. (1995). Language acquisition. In L. R. Gleitman, M. Liberman & D. N. Osherson, (Eds.), *An Invitation to Cognitive Science, Vol. 1* (pp. 107–208). MIT Press.

Rickford, J. R. (1996). Copula variability in Jamaican Creole and African American Vernacular English: A reanalysis of DeCamp's texts. In G. R. Guy, C. Feagin, D. Schiffrin & J. Baugh (Eds.), *Towards a social science of language. Vol. 1: Variation and change in language and society* (pp. 357–372). John Benjamins.

Rickford, J. R. (1999). *African American vernacular English: Features, evolution, educational implications*. Blackwell.

Rickford, J. R., & Rickford, A. E. (1995). Dialect readers revisited. *Linguistics and Education*, 7(2), 107–128.

Robinson, J. (2019). British accents and dialects: Received pronunciation. *British Library*, April 24. https://www.bl.uk/british-accents-and-dialects/articles/received-pronunciation

Romaine, S., & Lange, D. (1991). The use of like as a marker of reported speech and thought: A case of grammaticalization in progress. *American Speech*, 66(3), 227–279.

Ruiz, R. (1990). Official languages and language planning. In K. L. Adams & D. T. Brink (Eds.), *Perspectives on official English: The campaign for English as the official language of the USA* (pp. 11–24). Mouton de Gruyter.

Ryan, E. B., Giles, H., & Sebastian, R. J. (1982). An integrative perspective for the study of attitudes toward language variation. In E. B. Ryan & H. Giles (Eds.), *Attitudes towards language variation: Social and applied contexts* (pp. 1–19). Edward Arnold.

Sankin Speech Improvement. (2020). What is upspeak? https://www.sankinspeechimprovement.com/are-you-asking-me-or-telling-me-speech-pattern/

Sapir, E. (1924). The unconscious patterning of behavior in society. In E. S. Dummer (Ed.), *The Unconscious: A symposium* (pp. 114–142). Knopf.

Scarborough, H., & Wyckoff, J. (1986). Mother, I'd still rather do it myself: Some further non effects of "motherese." *Journal of Child Language,* 13(2), 431–437.

Schieffelin, B. B. (1990). *The give and take of everyday life: Language, socialization of Kaluli children.* Cambridge University Press.

Schieffelin, B. B., & Ochs, E. (1986). Language socialization. *Annual Review of Anthropology,* 15(1), 163–191.

Silverman, D., Blankenship, B., Kirk, P., & Ladefoged, P. (1995). Phonetic structures in Jalapa Mazatec. *Anthropological Linguistics,* 37, 70–88.

Skinner, B. F. (1957/2008). *Verbal behavior.* Echo Point Books and Media.

Sterponi, L. (2010). Learning communicative competence. In D. F. Lancy, J. Bock & S. Gaskins (Eds.), *The anthropology of learning in childhood* (pp. 235–259). Rowman & Littlefield.

Supreme Court of Iowa. (1921). State v. Bartels. *Iowa Reports* 191: 1060–1080.

Tagliamonte, S., & D'Arcy, A. (2004). He's like, she's like: The quotative system in Canadian youth. *Journal of Sociolinguistics,* 8(4), 493–514.

Tagliamonte, S., & Hudson, R. (1999). *Be like* et al. beyond America: The quotative system in British and Canadian youth. *Journal of Sociolinguistics,* 3(2), 147–172.

Takaki, R. (2008). *A different mirror: A history of multicultural America.* Back Bay Books.

Tannen, D. (1990). *You just don't understand: Women and men in conversation.* William Morrow.

Thirty Million Words Initiative. (2015). Thirty million words: Meet Shurand. https://youtu.be/IOFnRoUiO6Y

Tieken-Boon van Ostade, I. (2010). Lowth as an icon of prescriptivism. In R. Hickey (Ed.), *Eighteenth-Century English: Ideology and change* (pp. 73–88). Cambridge University Press.

Tomasello, M. (2000). First steps toward a usage-based theory of language acquisition. *Cognitive Linguistics,* 11(1/2), 61–82.

Tomlinson, J. M., & Tree, J. E. (2011). Listeners' comprehension of uptalk in spontaneous speech. *Cognition,* 119(1), 58–69.

Valdés, G. (2004). Between support and marginalization: The development of academic language in linguistic minority children. *International Journal of Bilingual Education and Bilingualism,* 7(2/3), 102–132.

Vélez-Ibáñez, C. G., & Greenberg, J. B. (1992). Formation and transformation of funds of knowledge among U.S. Mexican households. *Anthropology & Education Quarterly,* 23(4), 313–335.

Watson-Gegeo, K. (1992). Thick explanation in the ethnographic study of child socialization: A longitudinal study of the problem of schooling for Kwara'ae (Solomon Islands) children. *New Directions for Child Development,* 58, 51–66.

Wolf, N. (2011). Young women, give up the vocal fry and reclaim your strong female voice. *The Guardian,* July 24. https://www.theguardian.com/commentisfree/2015/jul/24/vocal-fry-strong-female-voice

Wolfram, W. (1974). *Sociolinguistic aspects of assimilation: Puerto Rican English in New York City*. Center for Applied Linguistics.

Wolfram, W., & Christian, D. (1976). *Appalachian speech*. Center for Applied Linguistics.

Wolfram, W., & Thomas, E. (2002). *The development of African American English*. Blackwell.

Wolk, L., Abdelli-Beruh, N. B., & Slavin, D. (2012). Habitual use of vocal fry in young adult female speakers. *Journal of Voice*, 26(3), 111–116.

Woolard, K. (1992). Language ideology: Issues and approaches. *Pragmatics*, 2(3), 235–249.

Woolard, K. (1998). Introduction: Language ideology as a field of inquiry. In B. B. Schieffelin, K. Woolard, & P. Krositsky (Eds.), *Language ideologies: Practice and theory* (pp. 3–50). Oxford University Press.

Woolard, K. A., & Scheiffelin, B. B. (1994). Language ideology. *Annual Review of Anthropology*, 23, 55–82.

Zentella, A. C. (1997). *Growing up bilingual: Puerto Rican children in New York*. Blackwell.

Zentella, A. C. (2005). Premises, promises, and pitfalls of language socialization research in Latino families and communities. In A. C. Zentella (´), *Building on strength: Language and literacy in Latino families and communities* (pp. 13–30). Teachers College Press.

3

WHAT'S PAST IS PROLOGUE

Language Deficit Research Past and Present

with Darrin Hetrick

In a promotional video for President Barack Obama's Early Learning Initiative, he makes the following claim: "We know that right now, during the first three years of life, a child born into a low-income family, hears 30 million fewer words than a child born into a well-off family" (Obama, 2014; also quoted by the U.S. Department of Education, 2015). In another speech on the state of the U.S. economy, he reiterates the claim, further emphasizing that "by the time [the child] starts school, she's already behind. And that deficit can compound itself over time" (Washington Post, 2013). The number Obama cites (30 million) is from the influential Hart & Risley (1995) study, but the notion that working-class and lower-class children suffer from linguistic – and, therefore, potentially cognitive – impoverishment has a longer history, going back to (at least) Bernstein (1966) and Bereiter & Engelmann (1966). As was described in Chapter 2, research in (socio)linguistics and anthropology has demonstrated the complexity of human language and interaction across cultures and social classes. Yet, debatable research findings from language gap studies have become so popular, they are often accepted as fact, even by a U.S. president. Today, language gap research has become a cottage industry, and both individual researchers and large-scale initiatives (Providence Talks, Thirty Million Words) are funded by wealthy donors (like Michael Bloomberg: Bloomberg Philanthropies, 2019), private organizations (e.g., Clinton Foundation, 2014), and public sources (e.g., U.S. Department of Health and Human Services, 2017).

This chapter reviews the major theories, methods, and findings within language gap research. We examine how deficit theories and proposals in the 1960s and 1970s paved the way for a resurgence in language gap studies. We argue that the new wave of language gap research is connected to language deficit research of the past, thus re-forming conceptualizations of linguistic deficits for a new generation of marginalized youth. Our critique is guided by the following observations: 1) despite claims like Obama's, the findings of language gap studies are actually inconsistent; 2) most language gap studies lack a theoretical foundation in the language sciences; 3) most language gap studies lack an operational definition of "language" that reflects research in linguistics; 4) most language gap studies do not consider dialectal diversity; and 5) by focusing on "gaps," instead of the human capacity for language, the linguistic resources of children are ignored.

The Prologue: Theoretical Bases of Language Deficit Ideology

Basil Bernstein proposed the theory of *elaborated* and *restricted codes* in 1966, developing the ideas further in a series of publications (see Bernstein, 1971) in which he argues for a connection between language, social class, and educational success. He characterizes the language of the working class as a *restricted code*, which is predictable, contains simple and rigid syntax, and makes it difficult to express abstract concepts. Middle-class speakers, on the other hand, speak an *elaborated code*, which is less predictable, requires more complex planning, and exhibits more complex syntax. Bernstein's conclusions were based on audio-recorded interviews with working- and middle-class youth from a London day college, all of whom were "messenger boys" who came from unskilled and semi-skilled backgrounds. For example, one experiment involved boys aged 15–18, who were prompted to discuss "the abolition of capital punishment" (1971, p. 83). As Labov (1972) points out, Bernstein does not control for the research participants' perceptions of the test stimuli and, thus, they may have interpreted them as requests for information, commands for action, threats, or meaningless sequences of words: "With human subjects, it is absurd to believe that identical stimuli are obtained by asking everyone the same question" (p. 221). This is exactly the type of stilted speech data that Labov warns against.

Interestingly, Bernstein and Labov make similar observations about middle-class speech – it is more verbose and filled with phrases with limited semantic impact such as frequent use of "I think." However, they draw different conclusions about what this contributes to the meaning of the utterance. Labov (1972) argues that the verbosity of the middle-class speaker is marked by excessive padding, which creates the *impression* that someone is educated without demonstrating complex thought. Bernstein, on the other hand, portrays middle-class speech in more glowing terms. For example, the frequent hesitation pauses are not interpreted as disfluencies, which interrupt the flow of speech (Corley & Stewart, 2008), or discourse markers, that signal the speaker needs more time to think of what to say, both of which are plausible interpretations (Swerts, 1997). Instead, Bernstein concludes that the pauses give middle-class speakers time to consider a wider range of syntactic alternatives in their elaborated code. While this interpretation is not out of the realm of possibilities, Bernstein never considers a simpler explanation for the pauses: The speaker is simply unsure about what to say.

Bernstein was motivated by the educational challenges of working-class youth who did not experience the educational success of their middle-class peers, and, like many of the proposals that followed, he theorized that language was to blame. In writing about his results, he emphasizes that his intention is not to devalue the speech of lower-class speakers, and stresses that the codes refer to performance not competence (in a Chomskyan sense), and therefore are not related to linguistic ability (Bernstein, 1986, p. 474). For example, he argues that the "restricted code contains a vast potential of meanings" and "should not be disvalued" and that schools must do more to understand these students and, presumably, their restricted code (Bernstein, 1971, p. 117). In some ways, then, Bernstein's research aligns with linguistic anthropological work suggesting that there is a mismatch between the language spoken at home and that which is expected in schools (e.g., Heath, 1983; Philips, 1983).

However, while he rejects the characterization, Bernstein must be considered an important contributor to deficit ideology. It is difficult to interpret claims like the following in any other way:

> Where children are limited to a restricted code, primarily because of the subculture and role systems of the family, community, and work, we can expect a major problem of educability whose source lies not in the genetic code but in the culturally determined communication code.
>
> *(Bernstein, 1971, p. 151)*

He further emphasizes "the relative backwardness of many working-class children who live in areas of high population density or in rural areas may well be culturally induced backwardness transmitted by the linguistic process" (p. 151). While Bernstein argues that all humans have the same potential, and the production of the specific code is not correlated with non-verbal IQ test scores, he claims that because lower-class children are enculturated into (and through) a restricted code, they lack the linguistic resources to be educated effectively and are trapped in their restricted code. Such claims allude to the theory of linguistic determinism and, indeed, Bernstein describes how he "chased" that body of literature (e.g. Sapir, 1956).

As a neo-Marxist, Bernstein (1971) he was primarily concerned with the impact of class status on language development and educational equity, and does not include race in his analyses. However, he does periodically allude to race, for example when discussing the U.S. Civil Rights movement: "The language of social protest, with its challenging assumptions, its grasping towards new cultural forms, may play an important role in breaking down the limitations of sub-culturally bound restricted codes" (p. 162). This argument suggests that he views the language of African Americans as a restricted code that is sub-culturally bound, even if the Civil Rights movement may end up liberating them from their linguistic limitations.

With a similar focus on class differences in language use, but in the United States, Bereiter & Engelmann (1966) claim that poor children – and their focus is Black kids – suffer from intellectual backwardness and speak a non-logical mode of expression. Based on interviews conducted with children, they argue that the culprit for the intellectual inferiority of lower-class kids is cultural deprivation, which results from lacking the necessary knowledge and ability to be successful in school. They are "deprived of that part of culture that can only be acquired through teaching…[they] may not even learn how to be taught" (p. 33). The main cause of cultural deprivation, as they argue, is verbal deprivation. Lower-class children are exposed to language that lacks cognitive use and is simply illogical: "With no known exceptions, studies of three to five-year old children from lower socio-economic backgrounds have shown them to be retarded or below average in every intellectual ability" (pp. 3–4).

To make their case, Bereiter and Engelmann proffer a series of examples as illustration. They use the term "giant word syndrome" to describe the children's inability to express sentences as sequences of meaningful parts, creating a giant word instead of a sentence (p. 34); example utterances demonstrating this include "He bih daw" for "He's a big dog" and "Uai-ga-na-ju" for "I ain't got no juice." In characterizing this as "giant word syndrome," they ignore the fact that while a sentence of written English uses gaps between individual words, there are no little silences between words in the natural stream of speech. One word runs seamlessly into the next, and therefore all humans exhibit what they call giant word syndrome.

Another perplexing argument involves the acquisition of words. Bereiter and Engelmann suggest that the culturally privileged child acquires the knowledge that sentences are made up of words very early, while culturally deprived children simply approximate "noises." Evidence for this assertion emerges from interviews with children in which they ask the question, "What's another way of saying 'green and red'?" The correct answer they expect is "red and green," but because some children simply repeated the phrase "green and red" instead of alternating the nouns, they concluded that "green and red" was understood as a three-syllable word, with unalterable components. One can only speculate about how the children interpreted such strange and stilted questions, conducted in laboratories by older White researchers. At the very least, we can speculate that the speech data they gathered were impacted by the conditions in which they were collected. Furthermore, the interpretation that the children did not interpret "red," "green," and "and" as separate words would immediately be contradicted as soon as they heard the kid using any of those words (separately) in a different context. Did they? It would be shocking if they did not, but we don't know because Bereiter and Engelmann did not publish much of their data.

Another example that demonstrates a phonological misinterpretation is the claim that the children pronounce the words *it, is, in,* and *if* all as "ih" (or [I]), rendering them homophonic. However, in a follow-up study, Steffensen (1978) found that while "it" and "is" *were* homophonous in the speech of Black children, the initial vowel sound in "in" was nasalized [Ĩ], demonstrating that the children had acquired and were obeying a phonological rule of assimilation (whereby a vowel that precedes a nasalized consonant is nasalized), *even when they did not pronounce the consonant.* This remarkable finding – which provides insight into how children acquire phonological rules without being taught – is obfuscated by language gap research that looks for, and inevitably finds, deficits. Because of Bereiter and Engelmann's lack of detailed transcription and phonological analysis, we do not know if their research participants also nasalized those vowels.

To overcome linguistic deficiencies, Bereiter and Engelmann propose a series of odd linguistic exercises. For example, they suggest that when teaching plural nouns, a teacher can place her hands below the table and ask a student "Where are the hands?" to which the student should respond "The hands are under the table." Putting aside the fact that this is an unnatural question – it would be extremely odd for someone to ask where their own hands are – the way in which this already unnatural question is phrased, is very strange. What person would say "Where are *the* hands?" and not "Where are *my* hands?" As Hymes (1972) and many others have pointed out, just because a sentence is grammatically correct does not make it a sentence that demonstrates communicative competence. Yet, Bereiter and Engelmann's suggestions violate the sociolinguistic norms of any speech community.

Like Bernstein, Bereiter and Engelmann note the mismatch between the knowledge and experiences that are valued at school and those that are valued in the homes of working-class kids. This claim is similar to those made by linguistic anthropologists who also pointed out this mismatch; however, whereas scholars like Heath (1983) and Philips (1983) place the onus of responsibility on the schools to accommodate linguistic differences, Bereiter and Engelmann blame the families. Like Bernstein, they argue that while lower-class children might have *other* (valuable) knowledge and skills not reflected in the school curriculum, "it does not matter" because the parents' "cultural deprivation" is passed to their children:

> Among disorganized and dispossessed minority groups, however, the culture appears to center around attitudes, interests, a style of life, and a scattering of unorganized beliefs and superstitions so unformalized that they may be transmitted without explanation, argument, or detailed exposition. Deliberate teaching is not normal or a necessary part of the adult role in such cultural groups, and neither the skills nor the language peculiar to teaching are developed and maintained. By contrast, in middle-class American society, as in most self-maintaining societies, nearly every adult can and does teach.
>
> *(Bereiter & Engelmann, 1966, p. 33)*

While their ideas might seem outdated at best, and interpreted as being influenced by racist stereotypes and/or raciolinguistic ideologies (Rosa & Flores,
2017), they were influential for the language gap research and educational policies
that followed. For example, pre-school was proposed as the arena in which linguistic deficits could be overcome, an idea that survives to this day in policies
aimed at getting lower-class children enrolled in pre-school as a potential panacea
for educational inequity (Barnett et al., 2005; Currie, 2001; Magnuson et al., 2004;
Reynolds, 1992).

Words, Words, Words

Labov's (1972) vocal and influential refutation of Bernstein, and of Bereiter and
Engelmann, signaled the ostensive decline of language deficit theories, which
seemed to follow in the steps of behavioristic theories of first language acquisition
that dissipated after Chomsky's critique. However, Hart & Risley's (1995) book
Meaningful differences in the everyday experience of young American children reinvigorated both lines of research. Hart and Risley contend that higher socioeconomic
status (SES) families talk more, with more varied vocabulary, while lower SES
kids experience a word gap. These findings were based on observations and audio
recordings, conducted for one hour a month over approximately 2.5 years in the
homes of 42 families (one baby each) from different SES backgrounds in and
around Kansas City, Missouri. They began collecting data when the children
were 7–9 months and continued until they were 3 years old. Of the 42 families
participating in the study, Hart and Risley included 13 higher SES children in
their "professional" category, 23 middle/lower SES children in their "working
class" category, and six children from a background of poverty, which they called
their "welfare" category.

   The participants included both White and African American families but,
whereas one of the 13 families from the higher SES ("professional") group was
African American, all six families from the "welfare" group were African American (Hart & Risley, 2003, p. 6). Additionally, there were three African American
families in the middle-class group, and seven in the lower SES group – 13 of the
19 families that represented the lower SES and "welfare" groups were African
American. Data collection involved 1-hour recordings in the homes on a
monthly basis, which totaled more than 1,300 hours of parent–child interaction.
They then estimated the average hourly rate of words to which children from
each SES group would be exposed (primarily focusing on parent–child interactions and ignoring other ambient conversations):

- professional class: 2,153 words per hour;
- working class: 1,251 words per hour;
- welfare: 616 words per hour.

TABLE 3.1 Hart & Risley's word count extrapolation (unit: million words)

Class	1 year	4 years
Professional	11.2	45
Working	6.5	26
Welfare	3.2	13

Based on these estimates, they extrapolated the number of words the children would hear on a weekly basis, calculated the children's total yearly exposure, and then projected it across the first 4 years as shown in Table 3.1.

Over 4 years, this results in a total of 32 million fewer words for children from the welfare category as compared to the professional-class group, thus the claim of a "30-million-word gap" by the age of 3 years (for a summary of the study, see Hart & Risley, 2003).

When describing the impetus behind their research, Hart & Risley (2003) state that "Rather than concede to the unmalleable forces of heredity, we decided that we would undertake research that would allow us to understand the disparate developmental trajectories we saw" (p. 4). This claim that there are only two explanations for the poor performance of working-class kids in school – genetics or a word gap – is reminiscent of a similar point made by Bernstein. While both end up arguing that genetics is not to blame, to propose it as an alternative explanation, even when rejected, turns a preposterous eugenic idea into a reasonable claim. At the very least, the portrayal of the problem in terms of a (false) dichotomy ignores the wealth of educational, linguistic, sociolinguistic, and linguistic anthropological research that proffers other explanations.

Since Hart and Risley's publication, there has been a deluge of research that has grown from a focus on a *word* gap to a more generalized *language* gap, measuring both language quantity *and* quality (e.g., Pace et al., 2017; Rowe, 2012). Following Hart & Risley (1995), many studies have found that SES correlates with the quantity of language spoken in homes (e.g., Gilkerson et al., 2017; Hoff, 2003; Hoff-Ginsberg, 1990, 1998). However, other studies have revealed variation in amount of talk by low-income families in both English-speaking families (Rowe et al., 2005) and Spanish-speaking families (Hurtado et al., 2008; Weisleder & Fernald, 2013). Sperry, Sperry, & Miller (2019a) provide evidence of varying amounts of words used within families from similar SES groups, and point out regions where children in lower SES families were exposed to significantly *more* words than middle-class families. Another notable study comes from Gilkerson et al. (2017) who used the Language Environment Analysis System (LENA) – a portable voice recorder that can be fastened to a baby – to replicate Hart and Risley's study on a larger scale. Whereas they did find a variance in "adult word count" between socioeconomic groups, their calculations demonstrate a 4 million (instead of 30 million) word difference between the highest and lowest SES groups (by the age of 4 years). They also characterize the variation within SES groups much differently, based on their finding that many high SES children experienced a relative paucity of input while many lower SES parents provide above-average levels of input. Despite what language gap organizations claim, they emphasize that "intervention is probably unnecessary for many low-income parents" (p. 261).

Defining Language and Linguistic Complexity

Conceptualization in research involves the refinement and specification of abstract concepts. The concept being measured in language gap studies is "language," but a problem arises when what is meant by "language" is words. A human child must hear a word to learn it and, thus, word learning is more like other types of learning, whereby a child is responding to environmental stimuli. However, other systems that are foundational for human language – syntax, morphology, semantics, and pragmatics – are ignored in word gap studies. Linguistic anthropologist Susan Blum (2017) has described "wordism" as a language ideology that regards language as primarily made up of units the size of words, which underlies most commonsense Euro-American understandings. For example, in language gap discourse, parents are encouraged to constantly name objects in their children's environment in order to prevent linguistic deficits, despite the culturally idiosyncratic nature of this speech event (for further critique, see Kuchirko, 2019; Paugh & Riley, 2019).

Using word counts as a measure of "language" is further complicated by what is considered a "word," which can be difficult to define and varies cross-linguistically. In polysynthetic languages, for example, it is often difficult to distinguish words from whole sentences because of complex morphological systems. For example, in Yup'ik, "Kaipiallrulliniuk" (one word) means "The two of them were apparently hungry." Furthermore, most language gap studies count only dictionary words but not private words, proper nouns, animal noises (Walker et al., 1994) or coined words (Hart & Risley, 1995); although Rowe (2008) does count onomatopoeic sounds like "woof-woof." While they may not be entries in a dictionary, non-standard vocabulary items must be learned by children, and stored in their mental lexicon. There is no justification provided for why such words are excluded – whether they are simply not counted for the purposes of the research or whether the authors do not actually consider them "words." By conflating "words" with "language," and number of words with linguistic complexity (Rowe, 2008), language gap studies utilize an inaccurate operationalization of what they want to measure (i.e., "language").

Huttenlocher et al. (2010) argue that the measurements used in studies like Hart and Risley's "are limited because they do not differentiate repeated use of the same elements from use of different elements" (p. 344). Instead of quantity of words, they assess the vocabulary of caregivers and children in terms of the diversity (variety) of word types such that different forms of the same part of speech count as one type (e.g., eat, eats, eating), and words with different derivational morphology count individually (e.g., quick, quickly). They also count proper nouns with multiple words (like book titles) as one type (e.g., The Little Red Hen). These discrepancies are important as newer research questions the claims from Hart & Risley (1995).

While Hart & Risley (1995) focus on the number of words, others argue that it is not just the quantity, but the *quality* of language that matters (although these are often conflated). However, the methods for measuring language "quality" can be diverse and potentially problematic. Some language gap researchers retain a focus on words as a measure of quality, including lexical diversity (Hoff & Naigles, 2002; Rowe, 2012), exposure to "sophisticated words" (Weizman & Snow, 2001), and the amount of "rare words" (Beals, 1997). Hart & Risley (2003) define language quality as including the quantity of "affirmatives (encouraging words) and prohibitions" (p. 8; also see 1995, pp. 95–140 for expanded description of language "quality" and parent behavior). Weisleder & Fernald (2013) use the vague description, "richer vocabulary and gestures" (p. 2143).

However, others focus on syntactic structures (Hoff-Ginsberg, 1999; Huttenlocher et al., 2010), the role of nonverbal input vs. overall amount of language (Pan et al., 2005), the mother's "linguistic skill" (Farkas & Beron, 2004), or maternal depression and reduced talking (Lovejoy et al., 2000). For example, Hoff (2013) argues that "In talking to their children, lower SES mothers make use of a smaller vocabulary and syntactic structures that are less varied and less complex, compared with higher SES mothers" (p. 6).

How linguistic quality is defined and measured varies across studies and, sometimes, it seems that researcher intuition is relied upon. Wasik & Hindman (2015) argue that wait time and open-ended questions provide superior input to children. Linguistic justifications for why these constructions are superior input are not offered, and instead we must rely on the judgment of the researchers. Yet, as was the case in Hart & Risley (1995), what is described as "better" tends to characterize middle-class norms, reflected in schools, but are not necessarily superior (or inferior) in any linguistic sense.

A few studies incorporate what we argue are more sophisticated measures of language quality. Hirsh-Pasek et al. (2015) find that, in exchanges between parents and children, joint engagement with symbols, shared routines and rituals, and fluency and connectedness correlate with "expressive language" as measured by the Reynell Developmental Language Scales. Also, in a study of the use of multiclause utterances among 34 children aged 54–60 months, Huttenlocher et al. (2002) examined the percentage of multiclause utterances produced by the children, their parents, and their teachers. They found that lower SES children both heard, and produced, fewer multiclause sentences at home and school. However, there was variability within SES groups, and the best predictor of the production was what children heard in their homes, *not* SES. In other words, SES was not found to be a good predictor of the use of "complex" syntax.

In a follow-up study, the researchers counted utterances heard by the child that were not directly addressed to the children, because "children sometimes reacted to comments and question that were directed to others, showing that such speech constituted input to them. In fact, it was sometimes difficult to determine who the caregivers were addressing" (Huttenlocher et al., 2002, p. 353). They once again found that SES was not significantly correlated with the production of multiclause utterances. Their conclusion is that input is important, and if children receive multiclause sentences in the environment, they will produce those types of sentences more and comprehend those sentences better. Nevertheless, they insist that much of what the children know about syntax cannot be learned from the environment; it's just that "input is required for acquiring a conventional system that captures such a structure" (p. 370).

Measurement and Testing Problems

Many language gap studies of language quality incorporate language assessments in ways that raise questions about reliability and validity. According to the Standards for Educational and Psychological Testing, validity is "the degree to which evidence and theory support the interpretations of test scores for proposed uses of tests" (AERA, APA, & NCME, 2014, p. 11). Validity refers to how test scores are used and interpreted, rather than looking at the construct of the test itself, and ensures that the results of language tests accurately reflect real-life language ability (Green, 2014). For example, a test may not be valid if it is designed to measure vocabulary development, but the results are used to assess overall linguistic ability. A benchmark of validity is ensuring that the assessment is being used to give evidence for only what it was designed to discover.

Test reliability, on the other hand, is the extent to which an assessment consistently produces the same results. Because language is both idiosyncratic and multifaceted, it is difficult to construct tests that reliably measure ability across a population (Green, 2014). What kind of language is being prioritized in these assessments? How well-trained and consistent are the raters? How do test-takers' characteristics or particular psychological state impact their ability on a given day? These are all questions that must be dealt with when determining reliability in language assessment. Because of the elusiveness of language test reliability, it is often recommended to use multiple forms of assessment to give a clearer picture of overall language ability. However, language gap studies typically rely on one type of assessment to make claims about general language ability, and the assessments are often used in ways not originally intended by the test developers, raising concerns about reliability *and* validity. As is pointed out in the *Standards for educational and psychological testing,*

When a test user proposes an interpretation or use of test scores that differs from those supported by the test developer, the responsibility for providing validity evidence in support of that interpretation for the specified use is the responsibility of the user.

(AERA, APA, & NCME, 2014, p. 13)

Such validation is not incorporated in language gap studies.

For example, a popular way to measure linguistic complexity in language gap studies is the Mean Length of Utterance (MLU) assessment (Hart & Risley, 1992; Hurtado et al., 2008; Walker et al., 1994), which is a measure of the mean number of morphemes (MLUm) or words (MLUw) per utterance. The MLU has proven valuable as an estimate of early language acquisition in children, a potentially useful measure of language impairment (Rice et al., 2010), and a popular developmental index for child language researchers (Rollins et al., 1996), and might be used to assess language dominance in bilinguals (Yip & Mathews, 2006). However, research on the MLU has revealed that it is *not* a valid measure of syntactic complexity for children above a very young age (Huttenlocher et al., 2002; Rollins et al., 1996; Rondal et al., 1987; Scarborough et al., 1991).

One problem with the incorporation of the MLU in language gap studies is the assumption that longer utterances are necessarily more complex. For example, citing an article by Rollins et al. (1996), Hoff (2003) argues that "Longer utterances typically include more content words and are of greater grammatical complexity than shorter utterance" (p. 1374). Yet, Hoff's claim is actually at odds with the findings in Rollins et al. (1996) who argue the exact opposite – the length of the utterance does *not* correlate with language "quality" – and point out that normally developing children show considerable variation in MLU test scores. For example, control of ellipsis and embedding – both of which are signs of syntactic sophistication as children get older – are not captured with the MLU, such that "At these higher levels, utterance length tends to reflect conversational context much more than developmental stage" (Rollins et al., 1996, p. 245). They conclude by cautioning against relying on the MLU to measure something as multidimensional as language. Another example comes from Klee & Fitzgerald (1985), who argue that the MLU is not a valid or reliable measure of linguistic ability nor a valid way to track changes in the child's linguistic system (pp. 266–267). They provide the following examples:

- *The big dog is barking*
- *She said he wasn't home.*

Both sentences contain the same number of words and morphemes, and would receive the same MLU score, but they are markedly different in terms of grammatical complexity.

Thus, the consensus is that the MLU may be a useful measure of a young child's linguistic development but: 1) it is subject to variability based on context and environment; 2) it should not be used to compare children; and 3) it is only useful for children up to about 2–3 years of age. Nevertheless, language gap researchers consistently use it to measure, and make claims about, syntactic complexity in older children, *and even adults* (Hart & Risley, 1992; Hoff, 2003; Hurtado et al., 2008; Rowe, 2008). For example, based on MLU scores, Rowe (2008) argues that lower SES *parents* have lower language skills and verbal facilities, suggesting that the linguistic deficiencies caused by poverty extend into adulthood.

In summary, language gap researchers utilize tests of language quality in the following problematic ways:

- they are not used as originally intended, raising serious concerns about test validity;
- they measure one specific area of language and not the whole of communicative competence;
- they tend to focus on receptive abilities only; and
- they rely on only a single assessment to try to measure the complex and multi-faceted nature of language.

Measuring communicative competence is quite difficult but different models have been proposed, including Canale & Swain (1980) and Bachman & Palmer (1996). As research on language assessment makes clear, however, there is no single reductive assessment that is ever going to deliver an accurate measure of "language quality."

Inconsistent Findings

If we are to believe Obama as quoted in the beginning of this chapter, and the institutes and initiatives that are devoted to curing the language gap, the research on how SES impacts language development is clear and consistent. However, while it is often portrayed as monolithic, there is inconsistency about the relationships between quantity of words, quality of language, SES, and linguistic development. For example, while Hart & Risley (1995) argue that the number of words is what matters, others find that the sheer quantity of words does not determine linguistic development: "The amount of talk directed to children may not be the driving force behind the differences in average child vocabulary size seen across social classes" (Pan et al., 2005, p. 776). Some find that SES predicts the quantity of words (Hoff, 2003) while others find the opposite (Weisleder & Fernald, 2013). Some find that child-directed speech, not quantity, is what matters (Weisleder & Fernald, 2013), while others argue that speech in the environment (i.e., not solely directed at children) is good enough (Huttenlocher et al., 2002). To illustrate some of the inconsistencies in language gap findings, we

TABLE 3.2 Inconsistent findings in language gap research

Finding		Examples	
a.	Quantity of words determines linguistic development	a.	Hart & Risley, 1995
b.	Quantity of words does not determine linguistic development	b.	Pan et al., 2005; Tal & Arnon, 2018
a.	Quantity and quality are correlated	a.	Fernald & Weisleder, 2015
b.	Quantity and quality are not correlated	b.	Cartmill et al., 2013
a.	Substantial child-directed speech is essential	a.	Golinkoff et al., 2019; Rowe, 2008; Weisleder & Fernald, 2013
b.	Child-directed speech doesn't matter – just what's in their environment	b.	Huttenlocher et al., 2002
a.	SES predicts language quality in homes	a.	Hart & Risley, 1995, 2003; Hoff, 2003, 2006
b.	SES does not predict language quality in homes	b.	Cartmill et al., 2013; Huttenlocher et al., 2002
a.	SES correlates with language quantity	a.	Fernald et al., 2013; Hart & Risley, 1995; Hoff, 2003; Hoff-Ginsberg, 1998
b.	Large variability of language quantity in same SES	b.	Gilkerson et al., 2017; Golinkoff et al., 2019; Pan et al., 2005; Song et al., 2014; Weisleder & Fernald, 2013; Weisleder et al., 2015
a.	SES correlates with syntactic development	a.	Huttenlocher et al., 2010; Levine et al., 2020; Perkins et al., 2013; Vasilyeva et al., 2008
b.	SES is not predictive of syntactic development	b.	Alt et al., 2016
a.	Imperatives are bad	a.	Hoff-Ginsberg, 1985
b.	Imperatives are good	b.	Barnes et al., 1983

provide examples of published research in Table 3.2. This is not an exhaustive list of the publications within each category; rather, the works listed are intended to be representative of conflicting findings in the literature.

Alternative Accounts: Sperry (2014) and Wells (1986)

The Hart and Risley study has received criticism focused on methodological and theoretical limitations (Baugh, 2017; Dudley-Marling & Lucas, 2009; Kuchirko, 2019), lack of sociolinguistic awareness (Arnold & Faudree, 2019; Johnson, 2015), cultural insensitivity (García & Otheguy, 2017), negative educational implications (Adair et al., 2017; Johnson & Zentella, 2017), and deficit ideological orientations (Avineri et al., 2015; Johnson et al., 2017; Orellana, 2017; Paugh & Riley, 2019). A detailed critique comes from Sperry's (2014; also see Sperry et al., 2019a) study of language exposure among children from different regions in the U.S. (Baltimore, Alabama, Indiana, and two communities in Chicago) – one impoverished urban, one working-class urban, one impoverished rural, one working-class rural, and one relatively affluent urban. The 42 children in the study were mostly European American except for the African American participants in the rural impoverished community. 20 boys and 22 girls were observed longitudinally from 18–48 months of age with an average of six video-recorded speech samples. In total, 157.5 hours of data were transcribed, analyzed, and sorted into categories reflecting the speaker and the intended listener.

Sperry highlights some important methodological distinctions between data collection for his study and Hart and Risley's. Hart and Risley began their study with the assumption that low-income children came from linguistically deprived homes and therefore needed interventions. Sperry's study focused on extant corpora data that were collected utilizing an ethnographic research methodology "to capture language in use situated within specific cultural groupings and the belief and value systems held by their members" (p. 90). The data in the original studies were collected during home visits but only began after the families felt comfortable with the researchers. Furthermore, whereas Hart and Risley discouraged talk from other adults during data collection to reduce the workload, natural interaction was encouraged in the original studies, and thus the language samples were more representative of everyday communication patterns. As Sperry argues, Hart and Risley's research methods lacked the ethnographic and cultural depth and nuance required to produce valid and generalizable evidence to support their arguments.

Sperry considered both child-directed speech and other language in the child's environment, which proved significant. While all children across all communities heard more vocabulary in the ambient environment than they heard spoken directly to them, the children in Black Belt heard the most, receiving 74 percent more vocabulary in the ambient environment than vocabulary directed at them. With detailed transcription of conversations, Sperry (2014) reveals how both talk directed at the children and talk within their environment should be considered input, since both are incorporated into the kids' actions and conversations – i.e., "Conversation is intricately woven in and around the lives of all whom it touches" (p. 293). Sperry found that *all* the children were bathed in verbal stimulation and that the number of words spoken in the five communities was similar, regardless of SES. However, in comparing his data to Hart and Risley, Sperry found that the poor and working-class African American children in the Black Belt of Alabama heard significantly *more* words – both in child-directed speech and in the ambient environment – than the other four communities *and* the professional and middle-class kids in Hart and Risley's study. To wit, the least economically advantaged children heard the most words.

Another important finding concerns variability in amount of language. Sperry notes wide variation in all communities, regardless of social class, which was dependent on situational variables – for example, the presence of older children, or significant events like birthdays. Many times, the number of words spoken in a single observation of a typically talkative family resembled the average number of words spoken in all observations by the least talkative families (p. 299). Due to such variation, Sperry points out that "[e]ven extensive visits cannot possibly reveal the range of any behavior in which people engage. They certainly do not allow the observer access to more than the participants want to be seen" (p. 300). Sperry concludes that the work of Hart and Risley represents an underestimation of the amount of vocabulary heard by children, regardless of SES. As Sperry notes, "The current study suggests strongly that the relationship between social class and vocabulary output is murkier than heretofore believed, and that the 30 million word gap is really only convenient fiction" (pp. 303–304).

Unlike language gap studies, Sperry considers sociolinguistic diversity, and points to the cultural differences in how language is perceived and used. For example, the lower SES homes, particularly in the South, valued narrative and storytelling, rather than book reading. However, in middle-class White American schooling, literacy is of the highest value. Therefore, this discrepancy could account for some of the academic difficulties for these children. As he explains,

> When all of these factors are considered, it becomes apparent that what the fiction of the 30-million-word gap has actually done is to cause us to forget old truths about children and talk. Children from diverse backgrounds may simply not talk, or not be used to talking, in contexts where mainstream children are comfortable with conversation.
>
> *(p. 309)*

Another study comes from Wells (1986) who conducted a longitudinal mixed methods study of child language development. His sample included 32 children in Bristol, England, with diverse family backgrounds. Individual observations of all 32 began soon after each child was 1 year old until their final year of primary school. Home observations were conducted approximately once every 3 months (10 for each child) up to age 5 years. A number of tests were given to the children at various ages to assess comprehension and usage, and the researchers interviewed parents to discover language philosophies and home environment. Researchers acquired more than 1,200 observations and a corpus of more than 250,000 child utterances. The data were analyzed both qualitatively (through discourse analysis) and quantitatively (including utterance counting and test scores). Despite the wide range of backgrounds and experiences of the children, he found a highly structured and systematic way in which *all* children produce language after their first birthday, regardless of SES. While these stages may occur at somewhat different times for each individual child, they tended to progress through the same sequences (see Table 3.3).

TABLE 3.3 Wells' language development stages

Stage I	Use of operators (there, look that, all gone, etc.). Functions – call (attention), ostension (direct attention), want, request. Limited grammatical resources.
Stage II	Appearance of limited questions. Curiosity with naming things. Emergence of grammatical structure (subject + verb, verb + obj., or subj. + object/complement) possessive structure.
Stage III	Questions well-established but only with rising intonation. Complete embedded clause. Verbs for mental states (listen, know). References to past and future events. Aspectual state – is it completed?
Stage IV	Integration of auxiliary verb into clause structure. Requesting permission. Explanation and request for explanation.
Stage V	Most major functions. Cohesion, explains habits (always), inception (starting to). Vocab of several thousand words.

Wells argues that progression through the developmental stages is guided by meaningful interaction with language that engages the senses. Children are not imitators of what they hear in their environment – they test hypotheses through interaction with adults and others who collaborate in creating shared meaning. One of the most striking results is the lack of clear differences in children up to age 5 "in their rate of development, in the range of meanings expressed, or in the range of functions for which language was used" (p. 142), regardless of SES. While there was wide variation in the quality and quantity of language used in the families observed, it was not connected to SES. Therefore, as Wells argues, "There is no justification for continuing to hold the stereotyped belief that there are strongly class-associated differences in the ways in which parents talk with their children" (p. 143).

However, once the children entered school, things changed. Even though by age 10, the oral skills of the participants were virtually the same, there were growing gaps in overall academic achievement. Literacy tests were the greatest predictor of academic success by age 7, which, as with the Black Belt community from Sperry's study, was less stressed among lower-class communities. Wells does suggest that "If some lower-class children did suffer from linguistic disadvantage, therefore, it was not in relation to their command or experience of oral language, but in the relatively low value placed on literacy by their parents" (p. 144). However, Wells does not blame the parents, but the general social context in which literacy in schools is valued far more than orality. Therefore, literacy knowledge at age 5 has an impact on later school achievement. Wells argues that there is an unequal value placed on solitary literacy activities, which overshadows the collaborative nature of speaking and listening.

Language Gap Discourse in an Echo Chamber

With a few exceptions (e.g., mention of Heath's work in Hoff, 2013), language gap scholars do not engage with the linguistic research on language socialization, dialectal diversity, or first language acquisition, and, when they do, it is often vague and/or misleading. This leads to opaque or questionable conceptualizations about what is being measured (i.e., "language"), which are not grounded in linguistics. This is a problem because, as Chomsky (1959) argues, "There is little point in speculating about the process of acquisition without a much better understanding of what is acquired" (p. 55). For example, Hart & Risley (1995) make this oblique reference: "We knew the 'anthropological studies' describing how children grow up in different cultures and different homes" (p. 22). However, Hart and Risley do not bother to review, synthesize, or interrogate the major findings from those studies, and a reader has to look at a footnote to discover they are referencing Shirley Brice Heath, Elinor Ochs, and Bambi Schiefflin, among others. There is no discussion about how earlier findings might inform or conflict with their research, and they apparently feel no need to respond to the robust literature on child language socialization. Contending with cultural differences in child language socialization would conflict with their proposal that one form of socialization is best, and thus the oversight might be strategic.

Furthermore, when first language acquisition research is reviewed, it can also be misrepresented. For example, a rare mention of first language acquisition theory from Hoff (2003) is presented as a false dichotomy between innateness and behaviorism: "One view is that development, in particular language development, unfolds following a genetic blueprint (e.g., Pinker, 2002). The alternative view, of course, is that the environment plays a substantial role" (p. 1368). Reducing the research on child language acquisition to two camps is a major oversimplification. There is no "view" that language is entirely innate – while Chomsky (1975) argues that humans are innately equipped with Universal Grammar, he also stresses that, "There is an obvious sense in which any aspect of psychology is based ultimately on the observation of behavior" (p.73). On the other hand, those who argue for a more substantial environmental impact also accept that the human language capacity must be innate. For example, Tomasello (2000), whose usage-based theory is a better theoretical fit for language gap studies, argues: "There is no question that human children are biologically prepared to acquire a natural language" (p. 247).

Presenting it as a false dichotomy ignores competing theories of first language acquisition (social interactionist, optimality, usage-based, etc.) and the complexity of the findings on how environmental input impacts child language production and which features appear to be impacted by input and which do not. While there is debate about how much the environment plays a role, there are no theories of first language acquisition that posit that it is either all nature or all nurture. As we mentioned in Chapter 2, the debate focuses in part on which features of child language are more and less receptive to environmental stimuli. For example, some syntactic features, like the structure of noun phrases in English (Lidz & Waxman, 2004) and position of the verb in Korean (Han et al., 2016), do not appear to be related to parental input or to rely on environmental stimuli.

Summarizing the research on first language acquisition, Han et al. (2016) argue that while children are highly sensitive to their language environment, language acquisition is "not merely a recapitulation of their input. Children acquire a system that allows them to produce and understand sentences that fall outside of their experience" (p. 946). Similarly, Crain & Lillo-Martin (1999) review experiments that demonstrate how certain features – like knowledge about syntactic ambiguity – "must be mastered in the absence of decisive evidence from the environment" (p. 59). On the other hand, Tomasello (2000) argues that the ability to creatively apply transitive verbs in novel places appears to be greatly affected by environmental conditioning.

Sociolinguistic research on language variation and dialectal diversity is also ignored, misrepresented, or misunderstood in language gap studies. For example, Hoff (2006) compares the language socialization processes of African American children as described in Heath (1983) to children in "sink-or-swim" language classrooms, apparently conflating first and second language acquisition. Her review of the research on African American Language (AAL) relies on research from scholars with training in speech pathology who focus on communication disorders (e.g., Craig & Washington, 2004) and completely ignores the vast body of literature on AAL published by linguists. Hoff's (2006) conclusion about linguistic development among AAL speakers reflects this omission: "The effects on the rate of language development are indistinguishable in the available data from effects of SES" (p. 64), thus suggesting that like low SES kids, AAL speakers will suffer from linguistic deficiencies, an argument that was effectively refuted decades ago (Labov, 1972).

Ignoring the sociolinguistics research can lead to methodological problems as well. Rowe (2008) relies on "researcher-directed speech" to compare parents from different SES backgrounds and declares that there are only two studies on how SES relates to language style among participants in "researcher-directed speech," apparently unaware of the body of sociolinguistic research devoted to how and why researchers collect naturally occurring speech data from participants from a variety of SES, racial, and linguistic backgrounds (Labov, 1972; Meyerhoff et al., 2015). Rowe seems perplexed about why the parents would vary so widely, apparently unaware of the history of sociolinguistic research that has sought techniques for the capture of naturally occurring speech data.

There is undoubtedly interesting work being conducted under the language gap umbrella, as the field of research is diverse and has produced a large number of scholarly publications. Still, most language gap researchers stay stuck in an echo chamber populated by their own colleagues and research findings. This critique speaks to the so-called siloing in academia, which is certainly not unique to this field. However, the repercussions are uniquely robust because, as we show in Chapters 4 and 5, they contribute to a discourse of deficit that blames minoritized language users for educational disparities, and they have a strong impact on popular language ideologies which inform media and public policy.

References

Adair, J. K., Colegrove, K. S. S., & McManus, M. E. (2017). How the word gap argument negatively impacts young children of Latinx immigrants' conceptualizations of learning. *Harvard Educational Review*, 87(3), 309–334.

Alt, M., Arizmendi, G. D., & DiLallo, J. N. (2016) The role of socioeconomic status in the narrative story retells of school-aged English language learners. *Language, Speech & Hearing Services in Schools*, 47(4), 313–323.

AERA, APA, & NCME (2014). *Standards for educational and psychological testing*. American Educational Research Association, American Psychological Association, & National Council on Measurement in Education: Joint Committee on Standards for Educational and Psychological Testing (U.S.). http://pediatrics.aappublications.org/content/pedia trics/134/2/404.full.pdf

Arnold, L., & Faudree, P. (2019). Language and social justice: Teaching about the 'word gap.' *Teaching American Speech*, 94(2), 283–301.

Avineri, N., Johnson, E. J., Brice-Heath, S., McCarty, T., Ochs, E., Kremer-Sadlik, T., Blum, S., Zentella, A. C., Rosa, J., Flores, N., Alim, H. S., & Paris, D. (2015). Invited forum: Bridging the "language gap." *Journal of Linguistic Anthropology*, 25(1), 66–86.

Bachman, L. F., & Palmer, A. S. (1996). *Language testing in practice: Designing and developing useful language tests*. Oxford University Press.

Barnes, S., Gutfreund, M., Satterly, D., & Wells, G. (1983). Characteristics of adult speech which predict children's language development. *Journal of Child Language*, 10(1), 65–84.

Barnett, W. S., Lamy, C., & Jung, K. (2005). *The effects of state prekindergarten programs on young children's school readiness in five states*. National Institute for Early Education Research.

Basso, K. (1996). *Wisdom sits in places*. University of New Mexico Press.

Baugh, J. (2017). Meaning-less differences: Exposing fallacies and flaws in "the word gap" hypothesis that conceal a dangerous "language trap" for low-income American families and their children. *International Multilingual Research Journal*, 11(1), 39–51.

Beals, D. E. (1997). Sources of support for learning words in conversation: Evidence from mealtimes. *Journal of Child Language*, 24(3), 673–694.

Bereiter, C., & Engelmann, S. (1966). *Teaching disadvantaged children in the preschool*. Prentice Hall.

Bernstein, B. (1966). Elaborated and restricted codes: An outline. *Sociological Inquiry*, 36(2), 254–261.

Bernstein, B. (1971). *Class, codes and control: Theoretical studies towards a sociology of language*. Schocken Books.

Bernstein, B. (1986). A sociolinguistic approach to socialization; With some reference to educability. In J. J. Gumperz & D. Hymes (Eds.), *Directions in sociolinguistics: The ethnography of communication* (465–497). Basil Blackwell.

Blum, S. D. (2017). Unseen WEIRD assumptions: The so-called language gap discourse and ideologies of language, childhood, and learning. *International Multilingual Research Journal*, 11(1), 23–38.

Bloomberg Philanthropies. (2019). Bloomberg Philanthropies announces replication of mayors challenge – Winning early childhood learning innovation in fine U.S. cities. Bloomberg Philanthropies, September 24. https://www.bloomberg.org/press/releases/bloomberg-philanthropies-announces-replication-mayors-challenge-winning-early-child hood-learning-innovation-five-u-s-cities/

Canale, M., & Swain, M. (1980). Theoretical bases of communicative approaches to second language teaching and testing. *Applied Linguistics*, 1(1), 1–47.

Cartmill, E. A., Armstrong, B. F., Gleitman, L. R., Goldin-Meadow, S., Medina, T. N., & Trueswell, J. C. (2013). Quality of early parent input predicts child vocabulary 3 years later. *Proceedings of the National Academy of Sciences*, 110(28), 11278–11283.

Chomsky N. (1959). Review of Skinner's 'verbal behavior'. *Language*, 35(1), 26–58.

Chomsky, N. (1975). *The logical structure of linguistic theory*. Springer.

Clinton Foundation. (2014). White House word gap event to share research, best practices among national experts and advocates with aim to close word gap. Clinton Foundation, October 16. https://www.clintonfoundation.org/press-releases/white-house-word-gap-event-share-research-best-practices-among-national-experts-and

Corley, M., & Stewart, O. W. (2008). Hesitation disfluencies in spontaneous speech: The meaning of 'um'. *Language and Linguistics Compass*, 2(4), 589–602.

Craig, H. K.., & Washington, J. A. (2004). Grade-related changes in the production of African American English. *Journal of Speech, Language, and Hearing Research*, 47(2), 450–463.

Crain, S., & Lillo-Martin, D. C. (1999). *An introduction to linguistic theory and language acquisition*. Blackwell.

Currie, J. (2001). Early childhood education programs. *Journal of Economic Perspectives*, 15(2), 213–238.

Dudley-Marling, C., & Lucas, K. (2009). Pathologizing the language and culture of poor children. *Language Arts*, 86(5), 362–370.

Farkas, G., & Beron, K. (2004). The detailed age trajectory of oral vocabulary knowledge: Differences by class and race. *Social Science Research*, 33(3), 464–497.

Fernald, A., & Weisleder, A. (2015). Twenty years after "Meaningful Differences," it's time to reframe the "deficit" debate about the importance of children's early language experience. *Human Development*, 58(1), 1–4.

Fernald, A., Marchman, V. A., & Weisleder, A. (2013). SES differences in language processing skill and vocabulary are evident at 18 months. *Developmental Science*, 16(2), 234–248.

García, O., & Otheguy, R. (2017). Interrogating the language gap of young bilingual and bidialectal students. *International Multilingual Research Journal*, 11(1), 52–65.

Gilkerson, J., Richards, J. A., Warren, S. F., Montgomery, J. K., Greenwood, C. R., Oller, D. K., Hansen, J. H. L., & Paul, T. D. (2017). Mapping the early language environment using all-day recordings and automated analysis. *American Journal of Speech-Language Pathology*, 26(2), 248–265.

Golinkoff, R. M., Hoff, E., Rowe, M. L., & Hirsh-Pasek, K. (2019). Language matters: Denying the existence of the 30-million-word gap has serious consequences. *Child Development*, 90(3), 985–992.

Green, A. (2014). *Exploring language assessment and testing*. Routledge.

Han, C. H., Musolino, J., & Lidz, J. (2016). Endogenous sources of variation in language acquisition. *Proceedings of the National Academy of Sciences*, 113(4), 942–947.

Hart, B., & Risley, T. R. (1992). American parenting of language-learning children: Persisting differences in family-child interactions observed in natural home environments. *Developmental Psychology*, 28(6), 1096–1105.

Hart, B., & Risley, T. (1995). *Meaningful differences in the everyday experience of young American children*. Brookes Publishing.

Hart, B., & Risley, T. (2003). The early catastrophe. *American Educator*, 27(4), 6–9.

Heath, S. B. (1983). *Ways with words: Language, life and work in communities and classrooms*. Cambridge University Press.

Hirsh-Pasek, K., Adamson, L. B., Bakeman, R., Owen, M. T., Golinkoff, R. M., Pace, A., Yust, P. K. S, & Suma, K. (2015). The contribution of early communication quality to low-income children's language success. *Psychological Science*, 26(7), 1071–1083.

Hoff, E. (2003). The specificity of environmental influence: Socioeconomic status affects early vocabulary development via maternal speech. *Child Development*, 74, 1368–1378.

Hoff, E. (2006). How social contexts support and shape language development. *Developmental Review*, 26(1), 55–88.

Hoff, E. (2013). Interpreting the early language trajectories of children from low-SES and language minority homes: implications for closing achievement gaps. *Developmental Psychology*, 49(1), 4–14.

Hoff-Ginsberg, E. (1985). Some contributions of mothers' speech to their children's syntactic growth. *Journal of Child Language*, 12(2), 367–385.

Hoff-Ginsberg, E. (1990). Maternal speech and the child's development of syntax: A further look. *Journal of Child Language*, 17(1), 85–99.

Hoff-Ginsberg, E. (1991). Mother-child conversation in different social classes and communicative settings. *Child Development*, 62(4), 782–796.

Hoff-Ginsberg, E. (1998). The relation of birth order and socioeconomic status to children's language experience and language development. *Applied Psycholinguistics*, 19(4), 603–629.

Hoff-Ginsberg, E. (1999). Formalism or functionalism? Evidence from the study of language development. In M. Darnell, E. Moravcsik, M. Noonan, F. Newmeyer, & K. Wheatley (Eds.), *Functionalism and formalism in linguistics* (pp. 317–340). John Benjamins.

Hoff, E., & Naigles, L. (2002). How children use input to acquire a lexicon. *Child Development*, 73(2), 418–433.

Huertas-Abril, C. A., & Gómez-Parra, M. E. (Eds.). (2020). *International approaches to bridging the language gap*. IGI Global.

Hurtado, N., Marchman, V. A., & Fernald, A. (2008). Does input influence uptake? Links between maternal talk, processing speed and vocabulary size in Spanish-learning children. *Developmental Science*, 11(6), F31–F39.

Huttenlocher, J., Vasilyeva, M., Cymerman, E., & Levine, S. (2002). Language input and child syntax. *Cognitive Psychology*, 45(3), 337–374.

Huttenlocher, J., Waterfall, H., Vasilyeva, M., Vevea, J., & Hedges, L. V. (2010). Sources of variability in children's language growth. *Cognitive Psychology*, 61, 343–365.

Hymes, D. (1972). On communicative competence. In J. B. Pride & J. Holmes (Eds.), *Sociolinguistics: Selected readings.* (pp. 269–293). Penguin.

Johnson, E. J. (2015). Debunking the "language gap." *Journal for Multicultural Education*, 9(1), 42–50.

Johnson, E. J., Avineri, N., & Johnson, D. C. (2017). Exposing gaps in/between discourses of linguistic deficits. *International Multilingual Research Journal*, 11(1), 5–22.

Johnson, E., & Zentella, A. (2017). Introducing the language gap. *International Multilingual Research Journal*, 11(1), 1–4.

Klee, T., & Fitzgerald, M. D. (1985). The relation between grammatical development and mean length of utterance in morphemes. *Journal of Child Language*, 12(2), 251–269.

Kuchirko, Y. (2019). On differences and deficit: A critique of the theoretical and methodological underpinnings of the word gap. *Journal of Early Childhood Literacy*, 19 (4), 533–562.

Kuchirko, Y., & Nayfeld, I. (2020). Language gap: Cultural assumptions and ideologies. In C. Huertas-Abril & M. Gómez-Parra (Eds.), *International approaches to bridging the language gap* (pp. 32–53). IGI Global.

Labov, W. (1972). *Language in the inner city: Studies in the black English vernacular.* University of Pennsylvania Press.

Levine, D., Pace, A., Luo, R., Hirsh-Pasek, K., Golinkoff, R. M., de Villiers, J., Iglesias, A., & Wilson, M. S. (2020). Evaluating socioeconomic gaps in preschoolers' vocabulary, syntax and language process skills with the Quick Interactive Language Screener (QUILS). *Early Childhood Research Quarterly,* 50(1), 114–128.

Lidz, J., & Waxman, S. (2004). Reaffirming the poverty of the stimulus argument: A reply to the replies. *Cognition,* 93(2), 157–165.

Lovejoy, M. C., Graczyk, P. A., O'Hare, E., & Neuman, G. (2000). Maternal depression and parenting behavior: A meta-analytic review. *Clinical Psychology Review,* 20(5), 561–592.

Magnuson, K. A., Meyers, M. K., Ruhm, C. J., & Waldfogel, J. (2004). Inequality in preschool education and school readiness. *American Educational Research Journal,* 41(1), 115–157.

Meyerhoff, M., Schleef, E., & Mackenzie, L. (2015). *Doing sociolinguistics: A practical guide to data collection and analysis.* Routledge.

Obama, B. (2014). Empowering our children by bridging the word gap. https://www.youtube.com/watch?v=NhC3n7oUm9U#action=share

Orellana, M. F. (2017). A different kind of word gap. *Huffington Post,* May 19. https://www.huffpost.com/entry/a-different-kind-of-word_b_10030876

Pace, A., Luo, R., Hirsh-Pasek, K., & Golinkoff, R. M. (2017). Identifying pathways between socioeconomic status and language development. *Annual Review of Linguistics,* 3, 285–308.

Pan, B. A., Rowe, M. L., Singer, J. D., & Snow, C. E. (2005). Maternal correlates of growth in toddler vocabulary production in low-income families. *Child Development,* 76(4), 763–782.

Paugh, A. L., & Riley, K. C. (2019). Poverty and children's language in anthropolitical perspective. *Annual Review of Anthropology,* 48, 297–315.

Perkins, S. C., Finegood, E. D., & Swain, J. E. (2013). Poverty and language development: Roles of parenting and stress. *Innovations in Clinical Neuroscience,* 10(4), 10–19.

Philips, S. U. (1983). *The invisible culture: Communication in classroom and community on the Warm Springs Reservation.* Waveland Press.

Pinker, S. (2002). *The blank slate.* Viking.

Reynolds, A. J. (1992). Mediated effects of preschool intervention. *Early Education and Development,* 3(2), 139–164.

Rice, M. L., Smolik, F., Perpich, D., Thompson, T., Rytting, N., & Blossom, M. (2010). Mean length of utterance levels in 6-month intervals for children 3 to 9 years with and without language impairments. *Journal of Speech, Language, and Hearing Research,* 53(2), 333–349.

Rollins, P. R., Snow, C. E., & Willett, J. B. (1996). Predictors of MLU: Semantic and morphological developments. *First Language,* 16(2), 243–259.

Rondal, J. A., Ghiotto, M., Bredart, S., & Bachelet, J. (1987). Age-relation, reliability and grammatical validity of measures of utterance length. *Journal of Child Language,* 14(3), 433–446.

Rosa, J., & Flores, N. (2017). Unsettling race and language: Toward a raciolinguistic perspective. *Language in Society,* 46(5), 621–647.

Rowe, M. L. (2008). Child-directed speech: Relation to socioeconomic status, knowledge of child development and child vocabulary skill. *Journal of Child Language,* 35(1), 185–205.

Rowe, M. L. (2012). A longitudinal investigation of the role of quantity and quality of child-directed speech in vocabulary development. *Child Development,* 83(5), 1762–1774.

Rowe, M. L., Pan, B. A., & Ayoub, C. (2005). Predictors of variation in maternal talk to children: A longitudinal study of low-income families. *Parenting: Science and Practice*, 5(3), 259–283.

Sapir, E. (1956). Linguistics as a science. In G. Mandelbaum (Ed.), *Culture, language, and personality*. University of California Press.

Scarborough, H. S., Dobrich, W., & Hager, M. (1991). Preschool literacy experience and later reading achievement. *Journal of Learning Disabilities*, 24(8), 508–511.

Shneidman, L. A., Arroyo, M. E., Levine, S. C., & Goldin-Meadow, S. (2013). What counts as effective input for word learning? *Journal of Child Language*, 40(3), 672–686.

Shneidman, L. A., & Goldin-Meadow, S. (2012). Language input and acquisition in a Mayan village: How important is directed speech? *Developmental Science*, 15(5), 659–673.

Song, L., Spier, E. T., & Tamis-LeMonda, C. (2014). Reciprocal influences between maternal language and children's language and cognitive development in low-income families. *Journal of Child Language*, 41(2), 305–326.

Sperry, D. E. (2014). Listening to all of the words: Reassessing the verbal environments of young working-class and poor children. PhD thesis, University of Illinois at Urbana-Champaign.

Sperry, D. E., Sperry, L. L., & Miller, P. J. (2019a). Reexamining the verbal environments of children from different socioeconomic backgrounds. *Child Development*, 90(4), 1303–1318.

Sperry, D. E., Sperry, L. L., & Miller, P. J. (2019b). Language does matter: But there is more to language than vocabulary and directed speech. *Child Development*, 90(3), 993–997.

Steffensen, M. S. (1978). Satisfying inquisitive adults: Some simple methods of answering Yes/No questions. *Journal of Child Language*, 5(2), 221–236.

Swerts, M. (1997). Prosodic features at discourse boundaries of different strength. *Journal of the Acoustical Society of America*, 101(1), 514–521.

Tal, S., & Arnon, I. (2018). SES effects on the use of variation sets in child-directed speech. *Journal of Child Language*, 45(6), 1423–1438.

Tomasello, M. (2000). First steps toward a usage-based theory of language acquisition. *Cognitive Linguistics*, 11(1/2), 61–82.

U.S. Department of Education. (2015). Bridging the word gap. White House Initiative on Educational Excellence for Hispanics. https://sites.ed.gov/hispanic-initiative/2015/05/bridging-the-word-gap/

U.S. Department of Health and Human Services. (2017). Bridging the word gap. https://www.acf.hhs.gov/ecd/child-health-development/bridging-the-word-gap

Vasilyeva, M., Waterfall, H., & Huttenlocher, J. (2008). Emergence of syntax: Commonalities and differences across children. *Developmental Science*, 11(1), 84–97.

Walker, D., Greenwood, C., Hart, B., & Carta, J. (1994). Prediction of school outcomes based on early language production and socioeconomic factors. *Child Development*, 65(2), 606–621.

Washington Post. (2013). Full transcript: President Obama's December 4 remarks on the economy. Transcript courtesy of Federal News Service. https://www.washingtonpost.com/politics/running-transcript-president-obamas-december-4-remarks-on-the-economy/2013/12/04/7cec31ba-5cff-11e3-be07-006c776266ed_story.html?utm_term=.773740f5770d

Wasik, B. A., & Hindman, A. H. (2015). Talk alone won't close the 30-million word gap. *Kappan Magazine*, 96(6), 50–54.

Weisleder, A., & Fernald, A. (2013). Talking to children matters early language experience strengthens processing and builds vocabulary. *Psychological Science*, 24(11), 2143–2152.

Weisleder, A., Otero, N., Marchman, V. A., & Fernald, A. (2015). Child-directed speech mediates SES differences in language-processing skill and vocabulary in Spanish-learning children. Presented at the Biennial Meeting of the Society for Research in Child Development, Philadelphia, PA.

Weizman, Z. O., & Snow, C. E. (2001). Lexical input as related to children's vocabulary acquisition: Effects of sophisticated exposure and support for meaning. *Developmental Psychology*, 37(2), 265–279.

Wells, G. (1986). *The meaning makers: Children learning language and using language to learn.* Heinemann.

Yip, V., & Mathews, S. (2006). Assessing language dominance in bilingual acquisition: A case for mean length utterance differentials. *Language Assessment Quarterly*, 3(2), 97–116.

4

TRACING THE GENEALOGIES OF LANGUAGE GAP POLICIES AND PROGRAMS

David Cassels Johnson and Eric J. Johnson

Throughout the previous chapters, we have leveraged the work from linguistics, sociolinguistics, and anthropology to highlight theoretical and methodological shortcomings in language gap research. In Chapters 4 and 5, we argue that language gap research, and the organizations and governmental agencies it influences, normalize the ideology of linguistic deficits. The impact of language gap discourse is revealed in the way that it is taken up by programs that affect families and children. In this chapter, we trace out ways that the language gap emerges across public policy statements, funding organizations, and community/family program contexts. As demonstrated below, for many organizations, Hart and Risley's work is the primary (or only) resource cited as "scientific evidence" for their program. We conclude the chapter by looking at examples of how the language gap ideology surfaces within public school classrooms and the education of students who come from multilingual backgrounds.

Language Gap Research Centers

Hart and Risley's home university, the University of Kansas, supports a program that builds upon their legacy, entitled the "Juniper Gardens Children's Project", which as its website states is based on "strengthening children's lives through science and community engagement." The project promotes publications, employment opportunities, and research projects that focus on the word gap (Juniper Gardens Children's Project, n.d.a, n.d.b). For example, one of its primary research projects, "TALK: Tools for Advancing Language in Kids," promotes language and learning resources for families, and boasts the use of "evidence-based practices to build the capacity of parents, early educators and interventionists to provide children with language-rich environments" (TALK, n.d., para. 1), crediting Hart and Risley as the impetus for the program (paras 2 and 3). The underlying deficit orientations towards language and parenting are explained in a statement on the "need for translating research into practice" (TALK, n. d.):

> The implications of *early language deficits* are serious as children who enter school at a disadvantage may continue to perform below their peers and may be at risk for language delays, poor school readiness and later literacy among other more serious negative outcomes including behavior problems, social isolation and the skills necessary to be successfully employed later in life.
>
> *(para. 5; emphasis ours)*

Research centers like the University of Kansas' Juniper Gardens and TALK project are examples of how the language gap continues to garner significant institutional support for programming and research that are founded upon deficit ideologies. The solution, as they argue, is intervention into the communicative patterns of families. As is common in language gap discourse, families – and especially parents – are the source of the problem, but also burdened with providing the solution (i.e., changing the way they talk to their kids). Nowhere is there recognition about other factors that research has shown to influence educational inequity – structural racism, poverty, health care, etc. (Delpit, 2006; Kozol, 2006). Furthermore, the notion that poor parents are less attentive to their children's (communicative) needs, lack sophisticated communication skills, and are thus less effective parents aligns neatly with stereotypes of poor people that have been engendered by neoliberal strategies, as well as the "culture of poverty" paradigm (e.g., Payne, 2018), that blame the poor for educational inequity (as well as their own poverty) (Gorski, 2012).

Although the University of Kansas' involvement with language gap research and programs is significant, one of the most widely publicized language gap programs is the Thirty Million Words (TMW) initiative led by University of Chicago School of Medicine professor and pediatric surgeon Dana Suskind (Center for Research Informatics, 2019). Suskind's TMW Center for Early Learning + Public Health "aspires to create a population-level shift in the knowledge and behavior of parents and caregivers to optimize the foundational brain development in children, birth to five years of age, particularly those born into poverty" (TMW Center, 2020a, para. 1). This charge is also highlighted on the TMW Center's homepage:

> We believe that, building upon a robust scientific foundation, we can create population-level shift in knowledge and behavior that leads to a future where all children start formal schooling ready to learn and thrive.
>
> *(TMW Center, 2020b, para. 2)*

The TMW Center's goal is to effect population-level changes in the way linguistically diverse parents communicate with their children. Yet, Suskind has recently acknowledged the shortcomings in the original Hart and Risley study, which prompted her to change the name of her research center from "Thirty Million Words" to the current rendition "TMW Center for Early Learning + Public Health." She even points out "the need to move beyond the idea, or even metaphor, of a 30-million-word gap" (Suskind, 2019, para. 7). However, the initial component of the center's name, TMW (i.e., Thirty Million Words) still stands.

Another example includes the Children's Learning Institute, which is supported through the University of Texas Health Science Center. The goal of this institute's Play and Learning Strategies (PALS) program is to "facilitate parents' mastery of specific skills for interacting with their infants, toddlers, and preschoolers that lead to better child outcomes, particularly in children from families with limited resources" (Children's Learning Institute, 2020, para. 1). Topics covered in the PALS intervention include a variety of language gap suggestions:

- attention to babies' and toddlers' communicative signals;
- supporting infants' and toddlers' learning by maintaining their interest and attention rather than redirecting or over stimulating;
- stimulating language development through labeling and scaffolding; and
- incorporating these strategies and supportive behaviors throughout the day and during routine activities such as mealtimes, dressing, and bathing, as well as at playtime. (para. 4)

While many children would benefit from these intervention strategies, they are not inherently superior to other potential strategies for interacting with children, and reflect white middle-class socialization strategies. With this type of "research-based" foundation, it can be expected that the instructional sessions presented in the PALS program will emphasize the deficit tenets that suffuse language gap research.

On a broader scale, the Bridging the Word Gap National Research Network brings together over 100 researchers from around the country to focus on the language gap (BWG Research Network, 2019a). The network is divided into work groups, which focus on (among other tasks) interventions aimed at parents, pediatric care interventions, and interventions for promoting language outcomes in children who are dual language learners. All of these interventions focus on "improving the quality and quantity of caregiver language" (BWG Research Network, 2019b, para. 1). It is also important to note that the research network is supported financially by the federal government's Health Resources & Services Administration's Maternal and Child Health Bureau (BWG Research Network, 2019c).

Political Support for the Language Gap

As mentioned in Chapter 3, President Obama's (2014) declaration that "a child born into a low-income family, hears 30 million fewer words than a child born into a well-off family" illustrates the impact language gap research. As part of the President's 2014 Early Learning Initiative policy, Obama solicited support for "empowering our children by bridging the word gap" in an official White House Blog statement (Shankar, 2014). In this blog post, the White House claims that

> Critically, what she *hears* has direct consequences for what she *learns*. Children who experience this drought in heard words have vocabularies that are half the size of their peers by age 3, putting them at a disadvantage before they even step foot in a classroom.
>
> *(para. 1; emphasis in original)*

The (apparent) impending academic doom caused by this linguistic "drought" is also related to additional social consequences:

> This is what we call the "word gap," and it can lead to disparities not just in vocabulary size, but also in school readiness, long-term educational and health outcomes, earnings, and family stability even decades later.
>
> *(para. 3)*

The message also pulls in other common language gap concepts that relate to brain development, parental interaction, and literacy:

> It's important to note that talking to one's baby doesn't just promote language development. It promotes *brain development* more broadly. Every time a parent or caregiver has a positive, engaging verbal interaction with a baby – whether it's talking, singing, or reading – neural connections of all kinds are strengthened within the baby's rapidly growing brain.
>
> *(para. 4; emphasis in original)*

In a promotional video for the Early Learning Initiative, Obama reflects on racial disparities that are frequently glossed over in language gap research, adding that "if a Black or Latino child isn't ready for kindergarten, they are half as likely to finish middle school with strong academic and social skills" (see embedded video in Shankar, 2014). We point this out to demonstrate how entrenched the notion of a language gap has become – here Obama conflates the word gap with academic difficulties facing Black and Latino students.

In addition to President Obama's calls to action, the U.S. Government has contributed to the visibility of the language gap in other ways. In 2013, the University of Chicago sponsored the "Bridging the Thirty-Million-Word Gap" conference held in Washington, DC (Bridge the Word Gap, 2013; Clinton Foundation, 2014). Among the conference organizers were the White House Office of Science and Technology Policy, the White House Office of Social Innovation and Civic Participation, the United States Department of Health and Human Services, and the United States Department of Education. These conference organizers were explicit about their orientation towards diverse language varieties:

> The day's agenda was designed to facilitate cross-sector conversations about cutting- edge research, interventions and technologies that could be implemented at a national level *to reach the large numbers of families and children who are among America's most affected by the impact of a language deficit.*
>
> *(Bridge the Word Gap, 2013, para. 4; emphasis ours)*

The U.S. Department of Education (2015) and the U.S. Department of Health and Human Services (2017) have been particularly active in promoting this stance, which draws from language gap research to support early childhood learning. For example, the U.S. Department of Education (2015) promotes "Engaging Families and Communities to Bridge the Word Gap" on its official blog. Included on this site are resources (tip sheets, milestone chart, bilingual benefits information) for families who "lack access to the types of information and resources that can help them make everyday moments into learning opportunities that are rich in language" (para. 2). They frame their suggestions for "bridging the word gap" by explicitly referencing language gap research – though, they do so without citing any specific "research":

> Researchers have found that some children are exposed to more language-rich environments than others during the early years, which can result in a gap in the quantity and quality of words that children hear and learn. The richness of children's language environment can impact school success and outcomes later in life.
>
> *(para. 2)*

The U.S. Department of Education (n.d.) also provides language gap resources for families, caregivers, and early learning educators on its website. The tips and resources listed on this site are also backed by un-cited "research."

The strategy of referencing "research" (without citing specific studies) as a way of leveraging credibility among language gap programs and organizations is very common, and demonstrates how the scientific validity of concepts like this are manufactured via word of mouth – instead of scrutinizing actual studies on the topic (Johnson et al., 2017, p. 11). By appealing to common sense, instead of citing research, governmental and other language gap organizations normalize the discourse of linguistic deficits (Johnson et al., 2020).

Health Organizations and Language

Framing linguistic deficits as a health issue is another common way that the language gap is promoted to the public in the media, research articles, and by national organizations (see Johnson et al., 2017, p. 15). In Crow & O'Leary's (2015) report on *Word health*, they describe "the word gap specifically, as not only a school readiness issue, but as a public health issue and the topic of a public health campaign" (p. 2). Speaking about the Clinton Foundation's Too Small to Fail initiative on closing the word gap, Hillary Clinton (2013a) explained:

> And the more I learn about the new research in the field, the more I am convinced that this is an issue vital to the future competitiveness of our country, the strength of our families, and the *health of our communities.*
>
> *(para. 7; emphasis ours)*

This type of statement resonates more broadly when backed by well-known health agencies. This is evident in the collaboration between Too Small to Fail and the U.S. Department of Health and Human Services (Administration of Children and Families and the Centers for Disease Control) "to develop a suite of resources that provides basic information on bridging the word gap to families with diverse backgrounds" (Clinton Foundation, 2014, para. 3).

The U.S. Department of Health and Human Services website, healthfinder. gov, includes a repository of contact information for health organizations. Among these is an organization called Zero to Three: National Center for Infants, Toddlers and Families (Zero to Three, 2020a). In addition to being a clearing house for publicly available information, Zero to Three also promotes its emphasis on influencing federal, state, and local policies, and posts open invitations to participate in their advocacy efforts. While advocating for enhanced programs and resources to support parents and families would be considered by most as admirable, the overarching positive agenda of groups like this can cause people to turn a blind eye to the way "research" is appropriated and used to push initiatives. Specifically, the language gap is among the topics covered within Zero to Three's (2020b) "resources and services."

For example, the discussion titled "Beyond the Word Gap" presents resources to "help parents, professionals, and policymakers understand the importance of supporting early language and literacy and how best to do so" (Zero to Three, 2020b). This webpage also includes a large infographic titled "Word Gap by Age 3" with a picture of a listless child, half covered in a shadow, looking down towards a hierarchically arranged statement (see Figure 4.1).

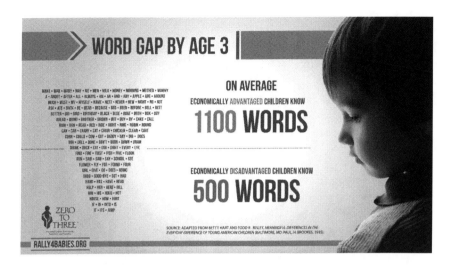

FIGURE 4.1 Zero to Three infographic on the word gap

Below the numerical statements, the infographic credits Hart & Risley's 1995 book as the source. Using Hart and Risley as a platform for discussing language development, the narrative of the webpage begins directly below the infographic:

> The "Word Gap" has come to symbolize the gulf that can separate very young children who have rich opportunities for positive early learning experiences from those who do not. Science reveals that early language and literacy skills are important predictors of later success in school—and that as a group, children in families of lower socioeconomic means have fewer skills and know far fewer words than their more privileged peers.
>
> *(Zero to Three, 2020b, para. 1)*

Although this is another example of a well-intentioned effort to promote early learning experiences, there are various assumptions that make Zero to Three's message seem almost commonsense. The opening paragraph of the website quoted above employs some interesting rhetorical techniques that draw on such assumptions. First, they describe the "word gap" as symbolizing disparities in "rich opportunities" between children – hence, children who lack "rich opportunities" must be relegated to having *poor* opportunities (i.e., instead of *different* opportunities). This is followed by the "sciencey" discourse phrase (see Chapter 5) "science reveals" to add credibility and authority to their claims, which they illustrate in the initial infographic by citing Hart and Risley. The final sentence connects the notion of "rich opportunities" to socioeconomic status such that it is easy to see how the "poor" opportunities of children from low-income backgrounds are described as resulting in fewer skills and reduced language skills.

The way health issues and governmental agencies are leveraged to proselytize language gap ideologies is also evident in national organizations that aren't related to the U.S. Government. In a 2014 "policy statement," the American Academy of Pediatrics (AAP) described literacy as an essential component of primary care pediatric practice. Before continuing, we want to be clear that we are not arguing against the promotion of literacy practices that support academic development; rather, we intend to show how the language gap has infiltrated the position of a well-respected professional organization like the AAP. That said, we want to look at how the AAP's policy statement compiles specific arguments that pediatricians should promote reading books with low-income families as part of their practice.

The American Academy of Pediatrics' (2014) statement begins by echoing familiar language gap claims: "Children from low-income families hear fewer words in early childhood and know fewer words by 3 years of age than do children from more advantaged families" (p. 405). They then connect this concept to literacy:

> Children from low-income families have fewer literacy resources within the home, are less likely to be read to regularly and are more likely to experience early childhood adversity and toxic stress at an early age, all resulting in a significant learning disadvantage, even before they have access to early preschool interventions.
>
> *(p. 405)*

This statement conflates the numerical word gap idea, a lack of reading in low-income households, toxic stress, and adversity – all causing significant learning disadvantages. The way that this statement randomly connects "adversity and toxic stress" to vocabulary and reading is disturbing. Toxic stress and adversity reflect contexts of adverse childhood experiences, a topic which comprises a growing body of research on physical and psychological abuse (Centers for Disease Control and Prevention, n.d.), and should not be conflated with everyday language patterns.

The American Academy of Pediatrics (2014) policy statement continues by narrowing its focus on literacy and health. To do this, the AAP points to Hart & Risley's (1995) work on the word gap, calling attention to linguistic and cognitive differences between "talkative" and "taciturn" families:

> Hart and Risley identified dramatic differences in early language exposure of 1- and 2-year-olds in low-income families compared with children in higher-income families. Cognitive and linguistic differences in children from talkative versus taciturn families were impressive by 3 years of age and persisted into school age.
>
> *(p. 405)*

Furthermore, relying on Hart and Risley's work (which, by the way, did not include a focus on literacy practices), the AAP points to language disparities between socioeconomic groups in terms of literacy patterns, and describes the impact of reading on linguistic features like the "complexity of syntax" (p. 405). After contending that low-income families have inferior language skills and lack literacy practices that could ameliorate the negative effects of this linguistic deficit, the AAP furthers the argument and suggests health-related effects of literacy activities. Specifically, it is stated that "Poor reading skills in adults are associated with poor economic potential and with the perpetuation of cycles of poverty, poor health, and dependency across the life course" (p. 405).

The AAP's indictment of language and literacy patterns in low-income families is punctuated by claiming that a lack of literacy ability directly impacts "health literacy," which they cite from the Institute of Medicine (2004) as "the degree to which individuals can obtain, process, and understand basic health information and services needed to make appropriate health decisions" (p. 2). In fact, National Public Radio reported on the AAP's policy statement as a call "to *immunize* kids against illiteracy" (NPR, 2014; emphasis ours).

The AAP's argument is a logically flawed syllogism: low-income families have poor health; they have poor health because they don't have adequate language skills; they don't have adequate language skills because they live in poverty. In other words, the solution is: changing language patterns will elevate families out of poverty and improve their health. This striking argument becomes normalized as commonsense notions about language patterns and poverty have become accepted as fact, and even a well-respected organization like the AAP can create such a definitive policy statement founded on language gap research. The structure of the AAP's argument essentializes very complex situations involving poverty, poor health, and substance dependency as grounded in disparities in language and literacy practices. Not only is this argument devoid of actual linguistic support, more significantly, it glosses over the deeply entrenched social inequities that exist between majority and minority groups in terms of access to economic, educational, and health services. Our point in this section isn't to dissuade pediatricians from promoting reading to low-income families; rather, we emphasize that poverty is not rooted in linguistic and cognitive deficits; it is based on broader systemic inequities that health organizations like the AAP tend to overlook and continue to perpetuate.

Philanthropy and the Language Gap

In addition to backing from federal agencies and large medical organizations, private philanthropic foundations have also ignited the visibility of language gap programs. Major organizations like the Annie E. Casey Foundation (2019), the Clinton Foundation's Too Small to Fail (Clinton, 2013b), and the George Kaiser Family Foundation (2019) have funded and/or supported programs based on the language gap. Bloomberg Philanthropies' commitment to the language gap exemplifies how large foundations have an immediate impact on public policies and programs. In 2013, Bloomberg Philanthropies (n.d.) awarded $5 million to Providence, Rhode Island to institute the program Providence Talks (2015). Recently, Bloomberg Philanthropies (2020) awarded funding to five additional cities to replicate the same program.

Providence Talks (2015) is program that tracks low-income families' language patterns by strapping a device on children that counts word exposure (see LENA, 2020). Based on the information gathered from the "word pedometers," intervention specialists make bi-weekly home visits with the families for language "coaching" (Providence Talks, 2015, para. 4). The Providence Talks promotional website outlines its rationale behind its focus on remediating the language patterns of low-income families: "research has shown that children growing up in less affluent homes hear significantly fewer words each day than their peers in middle and high-income households" (para 1). This familiar reference to "research" also states that

> This word gap quickly adds up. In fact, by the time a child growing up in a low-income household reaches their fourth birthday, they will have heard 30 million fewer words than their peers in middle- and high-income households.
>
> *(para. 2)*

In addition to actively broadcasting theses notions of linguistic inferiority to the public, Providence Talks also points to academic standards:

> Here in Providence, only one out of three kindergarten registrants enters the classroom at the appropriate literacy benchmark. Across our nation, we know that our teachers and schools work incredibly hard to catch our children up to grade level, often starting on the very first day of school.
>
> *(para. 8)*

The strategy of conflating language quantity with literacy practices was also demonstrated above by the American Academy of Pediatrics, so it is unsurprising that the same claims were taken up here. This is also reflected in the Georgia Department of Public Health initiative Talk with Me Baby, that claims: "The more words you speak, sing or read to your baby, the faster your baby will learn to talk and read" (Georgia Department of Public Health, n.d.). Although programs like Providence Talks and Talk with Me Baby are voluntary, the fact that they are promoted by city and state government offices demonstrates how language gap policies based on Hart and Risley's work manifest on a local level. This is further exemplified by local agencies that promote literacy by focusing on the language gap.

Literacy Organizations

As noted in the previous section, one of the most common ways the language gap is taken up by organizations involves claiming that diverse language communities lack not only vocabulary and quality interactions, but also books and opportunities for reading – which is assumed to contribute to a linguistic deficit. Libraries are prominent sites where language gap perspectives towards reading abound. The Association for Library Service to Children, a division of the American Library Association, offers shareable resources for its program Babies Need Words Every Day: Talk, Read, Sing, Play (Association for Library Service to Children, 2020). The ALSC launched its program by promoting a variety of resources that are "designed to bridge the 30 Million Word Gap by providing parents with proven ways to build their children's literacy skills" (para. 1).

Another staunch supporter of language gap programs is Scholastic Inc., a large book vending business that sells books and educational materials worldwide (and is heavily promoted in elementary schools – remember getting your Scholastic book order form?). In a partnership with the Clinton Foundation's Too Small to Fail initiative, Scholastic Inc. donated 500,000 books "to help close the word gap" (Scholastic, 2020). A quick visit to its website illustrates its take on language gap research:

> Research shows that the more words children hear directed at them by parents and caregivers, they more they learn, yet children from low-income families have significantly fewer books than their more affluent peers. In addition, researchers have found that by age four, children in poverty hear 30 million fewer words than their higher-income peers. These dramatic gaps result in significant learning disadvantages that persist into adulthood.
>
> *(para. 6)*

This statement provides a clear example of how the language gap is conflated with literacy. The initial sentence pulls from Hart and Risley's notion that quantity of words equates to quantity of learning, and then arbitrarily integrates that "children from low-income families have significantly fewer books" as a way to portray literacy as an essential element to language development. The statement continues with an explicit reference to Hart and Risley's familiar "30 million" figure, which is used to bolster the overarching admonition to read more books to avoid "learning disadvantages" in adulthood.

Reach Out and Read (2018), another nationally prominent reading program, highlights the word gap debate on its website and provides a broader perspective on language, parenting, and low-income contexts:

> We know that it is very important to guard against any suggestion of blaming poor parents for the circumstances of poverty, and that we should never equate parenting in poverty with poor parenting.
>
> *(para. 7)*

Reach Out and Read's stance on blaming parents for their own poverty, and poor parenting, reflects an explicit rejection of the "culture of poverty" paradigm. The website also provides links to both pro-language gap arguments (Golinkoff et al., 2018) and anti-language gap positions (Kamenetz, 2018; Sperry et al., 2019). Ultimately, Reach Out and Read claims that acknowledging the complexities surrounding the language gap debate "should help us to work toward a better understanding of what works to support parents, and to help them use reading together and looking at picture books to help their children grow and develop" (para. 7).

In this light, books are projected as an elixir to cure linguistic ailments. As Ana Celia Zentella has observed, "Parents who don't read to their children are accused of risking their children's well-being, and reading is portrayed as a magic bullet, a way to guarantee success" (in Avineri et al., 2015, p. 76). Zentella's point is that casting books as a "magic bullet" also diverts attention away from acknowledging institutionally entrenched inequities and biases that perpetuate the educational, political, and economic marginalization of linguistically diverse communities. Good intentions, in the case of these reading programs, are supported on the premise of linguistic inferiority espoused by the language gap. By promoting programs in this manner, the language gap remains unquestioned and continues to eclipse the deeper causes of social injustices confronting families from low-income and linguistically diverse backgrounds.

Language gap studies commonly portray reading events as superior types of parent–child interactions. For example, in Montag et al.'s (2015) discussion, adult–child interactions are looked at in terms of quality and quantity. Montag et al. point to limitations in everyday conversations and emphasize using picture books to prompt conversations between parents and their children. This position claims that "conversations are generally limited to here-and-now content, which limits the range of potential topics of conversation. Further, a conversation within an everyday context – for example, mealtime – is likely to have repetitive components day in and day out" (p. 6). While we recognize that "books are not limited by here-and-now constraints; each book may be different from others in topic or content, opening new domains for discovery and bringing new words into play" (p. 6), the value of alternative contexts for verbal exchanges for language development should not be overlooked. Reading books does socialize children into particular ways of using language (which are also reflected in school contexts), but other means of oral language use have also been proven to develop sophisticated narrative skills (Heath, 1983).

We understand that it is probably easy to read our discussion and think, "What's wrong with reading books to your kids?" We acknowledge this concern and want to emphasize that we do respect the wide diversity of literacy practices that exists, and we believe that reading books to your kids is obviously a good thing – it's just not the *only* good thing.

Before moving into our discussion of how the language gap concept surfaces within K-12 schools, we have assembled a list of organizations and some of their affiliations and initiatives that are based on the language gap (Table 4.1). This isn't

TABLE 4.1 Language gap organizations and their affiliations, initiatives, and projects

Organization	Affiliations, initiatives, and projects
University of Kansas	• Juniper Gardens Children's Project: https://juniper.ku.edu/ • TALK: Tools for Advancing Language in Kids: https://talk.ku.edu/about/
University of Chicago	• TMW Center for Early Learning + Public Health: https://tmwcenter.uchicago.edu/ • Dana Suskind: https://www.uchicagomedicine.org/find-a-physician/physician/dana-l-suskind
University of Texas Health Science Center	• Children's Learning Institute: https://www.childrenslearninginstitute.org/programs/play-and-learning-strategies-pals/
Bridging the Word Gap National Research Network	• University of Kansas: https://bwg.ku.edu/ • Health Resources & Services Administrations Maternal and Child Health Bureau: https://www.hhs.gov/cto/blog/2017/06/16/hrsa-word-gap-challenge-yields-lowcost-scalable-techbased-interventions.html
Bridging the Thirty-Million-Word Gap Conference	• U.S. Department of Health and Human Services: https://www.hrsa.gov/grants/find-funding/hrsa-16-040 • White House Office of Science and Technology Policy, Urban Institute, and the U.S. Department of Education: http://toosmall.org/news/press-releases/white-house-word-gap-event-to-share-research-best-practices-among-national-experts-and-advocates-with-aim-to-close-word-gap
The Health Resources and Services Administration	• Bridging the Word Gap grant competition: https://www.challenge.gov/challenge/bridging-the-word-gap/ • Háblame Bebé mobile app (grant winner): https://newsarchives.fiu.edu/2017/06/professor-wins-national-word-gap-challenge
U.S. Department of Education	• Talk, Read, And Sing Together Every Day: https://www.ed.gov/early-learning/talk-read-sing
U.S. Department of Health and Human Services	• Zero to Three: National Center for Infants, Toddlers, and Families: https://www.zerotothree.org/resources/series/beyond-the-word-gap
Georgia Department of Public Health	• Talk with Me Baby initiative: https://dph.georgia.gov/talkwithmebaby
Clinton Foundation	• Too Small to Fail: http://toosmall.org/news/commentaries/closing-the-word-gap • Scholastic, Inc.: http://mediaroom.scholastic.com/press-release/business-medical-nonprofit-partners-launch-new-national-effort-CGI-America
Bloomberg Philanthropies	• Providence Talks: http://www.providencetalks.org/wp-content/uploads/2017/08/playbook.pdf • Mayors Challenge Winners: https://www.bloomberg.org/press/releases/bloomberg-philanthropies-announces-replication-mayors-challenge-winning-early-childhood-learning-innovation-five-u-s-cities/
Annie E. Casey Foundation	• Campaign for Grade-Level Reading: https://www.aecf.org/resources/the-30-million-word-gap/

Organization	Affiliations, initiatives, and projects
George Kaiser Family Foundation	• Parent Engagement & Early Education Programs: https://www.gkff.org/what-we-do/parent-engagement-early-education/
LENA	• LENA "talk pedometer": https://www.lena.org/
American Academy of Pediatrics (AAP)	• AAP policy statement: https://pediatrics.aappublications.org/content/134/2/404
Association for Library Service to Children	• Babies Need Words Every Day: http://www.ala.org/alsc/babiesneedwords
Other reading programs	• ParentChild Plus: https://www.parentchildplus.org/the-word-gap-leads-to-the-readiness-gap/ • Little by Little: https://lblreaders.org/30-million-word-gap/

an exhaustive inventory of all programs and organizations, but we think it is helpful in demonstrating the far-reaching extent of the types of initiatives out there that are based on the language gap. These resources should provide a good starting point for anyone interested in learning more about how the language gap manifests in contexts spanning the medical field, literacy associations, government agencies, philanthropic efforts, and educational programs.

Views of Language Gaps within Education

The notion of a word/language gap is used so frequently, in large part, because it is conceptually embedded within larger discourses of social gaps and poverty. As McCarty (in Avineri et al., 2015) brings to our attention, describing the notion of a difference in words/language as a "gap" aligns with the mainstream way of portraying social disparities – hence, causing the concept of a language gap to resonate with broader issues couched in terms of a "gap." When applied within a K-12 context, the language gap is often discussed in relation to (the widespread) idea of an "achievement gap" (based measures of educational performance) facing minoritized communities and low-income students. This follows on from Hart and Risley's claim that the word gap causes developmental impairments resulting in low IQ scores. As explained by the National Education Association (NEA, 2019), "Test score gaps often lead to longer-term gaps, including high school and college completion and the kinds of jobs students secure as adults" (para. 1). Improving (i.e., closing) these types of gap is promoted as a primary concern by educational groups like the NEA, which ultimately results in the development of classroom practices. For example, the NEA provides strategies to "stretch" the vocabularies of students as a remedy to the achievement gap (Gilbert, 2019).

To establish the urgency of stretching students' vocabularies, the NEA points out "Statistics show that there is a wide vocabulary gap between our most at risk readers and our strongest readers" (Gilbert, 2019, para. 2). To support the claim of a "vocabulary gap," there is a link to "vocabulary research" listed at the bottom of the webpage. When clicked, the link takes readers to a website sponsored by the University of Oregon (n.d.) called "Big Ideas in Beginning Reading" – which explicitly outlines Hart & Risley's (1995) word gap research with multiple matrices describing differences in quantity of words heard hourly, weekly, yearly, as well as cumulative vocabulary statistics. The original NEA website on stretching vocabulary then proceeds to provide practical classroom activities: post-it vocabulary, vocab journals, vocab stories, word webs, showcases for abstract terms, and vocab parade (Gilbert, 2019). While these types of classroom activities can be engaging and effective when implemented properly, our point is to highlight the deeply intertwined ways that the "gap" discourse circulates within educational contexts. As demonstrated by the NEA, achievement gaps are linked to testing gaps, which are linked to long-term gaps, which are linked to vocabulary gaps – which reflects the same underlying language deficit premise in Hart and Risley's "word gap" concept. Essentially, this type of gap concept genealogy highlights the way that perceptions of achievement disparities are rooted in deficit ideologies surrounding language diversity.

Nowhere are the perceptions of educators towards language more prevalent than in contexts with high numbers of English learners and significant levels of poverty. In previous studies on language policies, the notion of language gaps was frequently mentioned (Johnson, 2011, 2014). In one case, an administrator described her challenges working with language minority students from a poverty background: "When you don't have a language, which many of our kids that are coming into us, they don't have a language, so there is nothing to build on" (Johnson, 2014, p. 169). This statement illustrates the notion of a gap in terms of an entire language; even though this administrator's students could speak Spanish, there was still a perceived gap in terms of not having the *right* language (i.e., English). This orientation towards language, either implicitly or explicitly communicated to students, can have immense social, academic, and personal effects on children, especially when they first start school (as described by the administrator).

In another context with similar linguistic and economic demographics, a middle-school history teacher explained his views towards his bilingual (Spanish/English) students. In his opinion, the benefit of being bilingual was overshadowed because his students did not speak the right variety of Spanish.

- I try to tell these kids that they're extremely lucky that they're bilingual, [but] I tell these guys you can know street Spanish, but you're not going to get a decent job. (Johnson, 2011, p. 15)

In this example, the language gap is based on the teacher's perception of the students' mastery of certain linguistic forms in Spanish. Even though the teacher himself was not a Spanish speaker, his views towards his students' socioeconomic background is conflated with his assumption about language forms within that community. Unfortunately, his statement exemplifies how these types of deficit views are often overtly communicated to students on a daily basis by educators.

Perspectives of what languages (and forms of language) are valid stem from broader linguistic ideologies entrenched through historical processes and perpetuated within everyday communicative contexts (as described in Chapter 2). In the case of bilingual and multilingual students, language proficiencies are frequently scrutinized in English and their home language(s). The commentaries of the educators provided above are examples of this process and reflect the notion of semilingualism (e.g., Cummins, 1976, 1998) – which was later reframed as limited bilingualism (Cummins, 1981). Essentially, the fundamental idea of these concepts is that it is possible for children who come from a multilingual background to lack proficiency in both (or all) of their languages – claiming that there are individuals out there who aren't fluent in any language (even their first language).

Researchers have since pointed out the flaws in this premise based on a variety of linguistic, social, and educational factors (MacSwan, 2000; MacSwan & Rolstad, 2003), and if you recall our discussion on language acquisition and language socialization in Chapter 2, it is easy to understand why this doesn't happen. In other words, if individuals can communicate effectively within their community (i.e., demonstrating communicative competence), they are linguistically proficient. Taking into consideration that language proficiency is generally evaluated in schools through standardized tests, it is more appropriate to examine reasons why linguistically diverse students struggle on tests, especially those that are usually: 1) based on navigating questions prompted through academic literacy, and 2) assessed according to narrowly defined communicative expectations of correctness. Even though Cummins (1998) has pointed out the negative connotations of concepts like semilingualism, the deficit dogma espoused by these concepts persists in education (Wiley & Rolstad, 2014).

As a way to counter these types of deficit orientations towards linguistically diverse students, Rolstad (2014) explicitly fleshes out the underlying influence of Hart and Risley's work on views of language within schooling contexts, highlighting, for example, that "their tacit theory about vocabulary reflects the view that 'English' is a monolith devoid of variety and variation, such that the list of words worthy of tallying could only be those included in a standard dictionary" (p. 3). In an ethnographic account of how the language gap manifests within pre-K-3 early childhood school settings, Adair et al. (2017) collected testimonies from educators (across multiple schools) who worked with linguistically diverse students from low-income backgrounds. When describing the challenges that their students face in the classroom, there was a consistent focus on *vocabulary* (p. 318):

- "The vocabulary is limited."
- "They're lacking the vocabulary."
- "They don't have the English competency."

- "Sometimes they just lack the vocabulary."
- "They haven't had the vocabulary with mom and dad."

Considering the swell of language gap programs and media coverage in recent years, these types of comments, while unfortunate, aren't surprising. The last comment in the list above is especially relevant to the language gap ideology (i.e., blame the parents). In an interview with another teacher, the role of her students' parents is emphasized:

It's difficult for [parents] to help their children because they didn't go to school very much, and they have limitations with language to help [the children], particularly in reading, some houses where they don't read a lot and the vocabulary is limited, that type of thing. When the vocabulary is limited or when parents don't have a high level of education, reading takes longer to develop because everything depends on vocabulary and the exposure to different things. And those are the things where I see more limitations.

(Adair et al., 2017, p. 319)

This is an example of how the language gap ideology manifests within the perceptions of well-intentioned teachers who see their students (and families) in terms of limitations, and judge them based on what they don't have. This example epitomizes the challenges faced by both teachers and students. The students have a sound linguistic system and are able to use language to accomplish meaningful communicative tasks (Zentella, 2005), but teachers often struggle to recognize this, and assume that their students lack basic language skills. In reality, a similar deficit could be said of educators who aren't equipped with the appropriate language skills to operate in contexts where their students excel. It is much easier to assume that the language patterns of school are inherently superior than to interrogate educators' working knowledge of their students' linguistic strengths and expect them to be integrated into classroom practices. The language gap casts a shadow over the practices of linguistically diverse communities and removes the responsibility of failure from the teachers by placing blame on the students' initial language environment at home.

References

Adair, J. K., Colegrove, K. S. S., & McManus, M. E. (2017). How the word gap argument negatively impacts young children of Latinx immigrants' conceptualizations of learning. *Harvard Educational Review*, 87(3), 309–334.

American Academy of Pediatrics. (2014). Literacy promotion: An essential component of primary care pediatric practice (Policy statement). *Pediatrics*, 34(2), 404–409. http:// pediatrics.aappublications.org/content/pediatrics/134/2/404.full.pdf

Annie E. Casey Foundation. (2019). The 30 million word gap: The role of parent-child verbal interaction in language and literacy development. http://www.aecf.org/resources/the-30-million-word-gap/

Association for Library Service to Children. (2020). Babies need words every day: Talk, read, sing, play. http://www.ala.org/alsc/babiesneedwords

Avineri, N., Johnson, E. J., Brice-Heath, S., McCarty, T., Ochs, E., Kremer-Sadlik, T., Blum, S., Zentella, A. C., Rosa, J., Flores, N., Alim, H. S., & Paris, D. (2015). Invited forum: Bridging the "language gap." *Journal of Linguistic Anthropology*, 25(1), 66–86.

Bachman, L. F., & Palmer, A. S. (1996). *Language testing in practice: Designing and developing useful language tests*. Oxford University Press.

Bloomberg Philanthropies. (n.d.). Past winners. https://mayorschallenge.bloomberg.org/ideas/providence-talks/

Bloomberg Philanthropies. (2020). Bloomberg Philanthropies announces replication of mayors challenge – Winning early childhood learning innovation in five U.S. cities. https://www.bloomberg.org/press/releases/bloomberg-philanthropies-announces-replication-mayors-challenge-winning-early-childhood-learning-innovation-five-u-s-cities/

Bridge the Word Gap. (2013). Bridging the Thirty-Million-Word Gap. Conference website. https://bridgethewordgap.wordpress.com/

BWG Research Network. (n.d.a). Bridging the Word Gap National Research Network. http://www.bwgresnet.res.ku.edu/

BWG Research Network. (n.d.b). Work groups. http://www.bwgresnet.res.ku.edu/work-groups/

BWG Research Network. (n.d.c). HRSA challenge prize winners. http://www.bwgresnet.res.ku.edu/hrsa-challenge-prize-winners/

Center for Research Informatics. (2019). Thirty Million Words. University of Chicago. https://cri.uchicago.edu/portfolio/thirty-million-words/

Centers for Disease Control and Prevention. (n.d.). Adverse childhood experiences (ACEs). https://www.cdc.gov/violenceprevention/acestudy/index.html

Children's Learning Institute. (2020). Play and learning strategies (PALS). University of Texas Health Science Center at Houston. https://www.childrenslearninginstitute.org/programs/play-and-learning-strategies-pals/

Clinton, H. (2013a). Closing the 'word gap.' Stories, October 3. https://www.clintonfoundation.org/blog/2013/10/03/closing-word-gap

Clinton, H. (2013b). Closing the 'word gap'. Too Small to Fail, October 3. http://toosmall.org/news/commentaries/closing-the-word-gap

Clinton Foundation. (2014). White House word gap event to share research, best practices among national experts and advocates with aim to close word gap. https://www.clintonfoundation.org/press-releases/white-house-word-gap-event-share-research-best-practices-among-national-experts-and

Crow, S., & O'Leary, A. (2015). *Word health: Addressing the word gap as a public health crisis*. Next Generation and Too Small to Fail.

Cummins, J. (1976). The influence of bilingualism on cognitive growth: A synthesis of research findings and explanatory hypotheses. *Working Papers on Bilingualism*, 9, 1–43.

Cummins, J. (1981). The role of primary language development in promoting educational success for language minority students. In *Schooling and language minority students: A theoretical framework* (pp. 3–49). Office of Bilingual Bicultural Education, California State Department of Education.

Cummins, J. (1998). Semilingualism. In J. L. Mey (Ed.), *Concise encyclopedia of pragmatics* (pp. 3812–3814). Elsevier Science.

Delpit, L. (2006). *Other people's children: Cultural conflict in the classroom.* The New Press.

George Kaiser Family Foundation. (2019). Parent engagement & early education. http://www.gkff.org/what-we-do/parent-engagement-early-education/

Georgia Department of Public Health. (n.d.). Talk with me baby. https://dph.georgia.gov/talkwithmebaby

Gilbert, A. (2019). Stretch their vocabularies. National Education Association. http://www.nea.org/tools/52083.htm

Golinkoff, R. M., Hoff, E., Rowe, M., Tamis-LeMonda, C. & Hirsh-Pasek, K. (2018). Talking with children matters: Defending the 30 million word gap. Brookings Institution. https://www.brookings.edu/blog/education-plus-development/2018/05/21/defending-the-30-million-word-gap-disadvantaged-children-dont-hear-enough-child-directed-words/

Gorski, P. C. (2012). Perceiving the problem of poverty and schooling: Deconstructing the class stereotypes that mis-shape education practice and policy. *Equity & Excellence in Education*, 45(2), 302–319.

Hart, B., & Risley, T. (1995). *Meaningful differences in the everyday experiences of young American children.* Brookes Publishing.

Heath, S. B. (1983). *Ways with words: Language, life and work in communities and classrooms.* Cambridge University Press.

Institute of Medicine. (2004). *Health literacy: A prescription to end confusion.* National Academies Press.

Johnson, D. C., Johnson, E. J., & Hetrick, D. (2020). Normalization of language deficit ideologies for a new generation of minoritized U.S. youth. *Social Semiotics*, 30(4). https://doi.org/10.1080/10350330.2020.1766210

Johnson, E. J. (2011). (Re)producing linguistic hierarchies in the United States: Language ideologies of function and form in public schools. *International Journal of Linguistics*, 3(1), E12.

Johnson, E. J. (2014). (Re)categorizing language-minority literacies in restrictive educational contexts. *International Multilingual Research Journal*, 8(3), 167–188.

Johnson, E. J., Avineri, N., & Johnson, D. C. (2017). Exposing gaps in/between discourses of linguistic deficits. *International Multilingual Research Journal*, 11(1), 5–22.

Juniper Gardens Children's Project. (n.d.a). https://jgcp.ku.edu/

Juniper Gardens Children's Project. (n.d.b). What we do: Language and communication. http://jgcp.ku.edu/grant-categories

Kamenetz, A. (2018). Let's stop talking about the '30 million word gap'." *NPR*, June 1. https://www.npr.org/sections/ed/2018/06/01/615188051/lets-stop-talking-about-the-30-million-word-gap

Kozol, J. (2006). *The shame of the nation: The restoration of apartheid schooling in America.* Broadway Books.

LENA. (2020). https://www.lena.org/

MacSwan, J. (2000). The threshold hypothesis, semilingualism, and other contributions to a deficit view of linguistic minorities. *Hispanic Journal of Behavioral Science*, 22(1), 3–45.

MacSwan, J., & Rolstad, K. (2003). Linguistic diversity, schooling, and social class: Rethinking our conception of language proficiency in language minority education. In C. B. Paulston & R. Tucker (Eds.), *Sociolinguistics: The essential readings* (pp. 329–340). Blackwell.

Montag, J. L., Jones, M. N., & Smith, L. B. (2015). The words children hear: Picture books and the statistics for language learning. *Psychological Science*, 29(9), 1489–1496.

NEA. (2019). Students affected by achievement gaps. National Education Association. http://www.nea.org/home/20380.htm

NPR. (2014). To 'immunize' kids against illiteracy, break out a book in infancy. *All Things Considered*, June 24. https://www.npr.org/2014/06/24/325229904/to-immunize-kids-against-illiteracy-break-out-a-book-in-infancy

Obama, B. (2014). Empowering our children by bridging the word gap. Promotional speech. https://www.youtube.com/watch?v=NhC3n7oUm9U#action=share

Payne, R. (2018). *A framework for understanding poverty: A cognitive approach*. aha! Process.

Providence Talks. (2015). http://www.providencetalks.org/about/

Reach Out and Read. (2018). Debating the 30 million word gap. https://www.reachoutandread.org/2018/06/25/lets-stop-talking-about-the-thirty-million-word-gap/

Rolstad, K. (2014). Rethinking language at school. *International Multilingual Research Journal*, 8(1), 1–8.

Scholastic. (2020). Business, medical, and non-profit partners launch new national effort at CGI America to help close the word gap. http://mediaroom.scholastic.com/press-release/business-medical-nonprofit-partners-launch-new-national-effort-CGI-America

Shankar, M. (2014). Empowering our children by bridging the word gap. The White House website. https://obamawhitehouse.archives.gov/blog/2014/06/25/empowering-our-children-bridging-word-gap

Sperry, D. E., Sperry, L. L., & Miller, P. J. (2019). Reexamining the verbal environments of children from different socioeconomic backgrounds. *Child Development*, 90(4), 1303–1318.

Suskind, D. (2019). *What cutting-edge neuroscience tells us about early childhood development*. Brookings Institute. https://www.brookings.edu/blog/brown-center-chalkboard/2019/09/26/what-cutting-edge-neuroscience-tells-us-about-early-childhood-development/

TALK. (n.d.). Tools for Advancing Language in Kids. http://www.talk.ku.edu/about/

TMW Center. (2020a). Mission. University of Chicago. https://tmwcenter.uchicago.edu/tmwcenter/who-we-are/mission/

TMW Center. (2020b). TMW Center for Early Learning + Public Health. University of Chicago. https://tmwcenter.uchicago.edu/

University of Oregon. (n.d.). Big ideas in beginning reading. http://reading.uoregon.edu/big_ideas/voc/voc_what.php#research

U.S. Department of Education. (n.d.). Talk, read, and sing together every day: Tip sheets for families, caregivers, and early learning educators. http://www.ed.gov/early-learning/talk-read-sing

U.S. Department of Education. (2015). Engaging families and communities to bridge the word gap. *Homeroom*, July 28. https://blog.ed.gov/2015/07/engaging-families-and-communities-to-bridge-the-word-gap/

U.S. Department of Health and Human Services. (2017). Bridging the word gap. Child Health & Development. https://www.acf.hhs.gov/ecd/child-health-development/bridging-the-word-gap

Wiley, T. G., & Rolstad, K. (2014). The Common Core State Standards and the great divide. *International Multilingual Research Journal*, 8(1), 38–55.

Zentella, A.C. (2005). Premises, promises, and pitfalls of language socialization research in Latino families and communities. In A. C. Zentella (Ed.), *Building on strength: Language and literacy in Latino families and communities* (pp. 13–30). Teachers College Press.

Zero to Three. (2020a). https://www.zerotothree.org/

Zero to Three. (2020b). Beyond the word gap. https://www.zerotothree.org/resources/series/beyond-the-word-gap

5

NORMALIZATION OF DEFICIT LANGUAGE IDEOLOGIES

David Cassels Johnson and Eric J. Johnson

In previous chapters, we leveraged the research from linguistics, sociolinguistics, and anthropology to examine language gap theory and research methodology, and how findings have been appropriated by government agencies, philanthropic foundations, and professional associations. This chapter takes a closer look at the connections between those foundations and the media, and their role in the circulation and normalization of language deficit ideologies. As was discussed in Chapter 2, language ideologies rely on broader prescriptive norms that influence attitudes towards different language varieties (and their speakers). Language ideologies encompass language attitudes (Ryan et al., 1982) but are associated with clusters of attitudes that perpetrate, and are perpetuated by, systems of power. Definitions for language ideology vary, but Woolard & Schieffelin (1994) offer a helpful summary and argue that a fundamental distinction lies between those definitions that take a neutral stance and others that take a critical stance, the latter tending to embed "strategies for maintaining social power" into the definition (pp. 57–58). Their definition builds on Rumsey (1990), who defines language ideology as "shared bodies of commonsense notions about the nature of language in the world" (p. 346). Language ideologies position certain linguistic features as more natural or normal, especially those popularly believed to align with prescriptive grammatical norms. Through language ideologies, hierarchies of language varieties are naturalized and imbued with hegemonic power.

Language ideologies are durable because of the process of *normalization*, whereby "a set of simultaneous or subsequent discursive strategies gradually introduce and/or perpetuate in public discourse...patterns of representing social actors, processes, and issues" in ways that privilege the linguistic and sociolinguistic norms of dominant speech communities and therefore lead to the "gradual normalization of key radicalized norms of describing the social, political, economic, [and educational] reality" (Krzyżanowski, 2020, p. 2). Language deficit ideologies are not new; however, we argue that a re-normalization of language deficit ideology is perpetuated by a new generation of researchers, public intellectuals, and politicians, as well as foundation and media discourse, which normalizes the notion that poor kids experience verbal, and therefore cognitive, deficits (Johnson et al., 2020). We reveal how ideological representation of minoritized families and their language varieties "come to be seen as non-ideological common sense" (Fairclough, 2010, p. 31).

The analysis in this chapter is grounded in critical discourse studies (Fairclough, 2010; Wodak, 1996), which provides a theoretical foundation for illuminating the connections between language and power. A prominent research methodology within critical discourse studies is critical discourse analysis, which is an interdisciplinary approach to discourse analysis that grew out of critical linguistics (Fowler et al., 1979), systemic-functional linguistics (Halliday, 1978), and critical social theory (e.g. Foucault, 1978). The dialectical relationship between power and language/discourse is a guiding focus within critical discourse analysis. A central tenet is that language is shaped by, and shapes, the social context; or, as Fairclough (2010) puts it, language "is always a socially and historically situated mode of action, in a dialectical relationship with other facets of 'the social' (its 'social context') – it is socially shaped, but it is also socially shaping, or constitutive" (p. 92).

While critical discourse analysis writ large is often described as a research method, it is not typically characterized by strict methodological guidelines, and a variety of discourse analytic techniques can be utilized under (or in combination with) the critical discourse analysis umbrella (which has led to criticism: Blommaert, 2001). For example, analysis of *intertextuality* has been proposed as a useful technique in critical discourse analysis and language policy studies (Fairclough, 1992; Johnson, 2016). Julia Kristeva (1986) coined the term (*l'intertextualité*) in her analyses of Mikhail Bakhtin's writings on literary semiotics, which popularized his mostly unpublished and unknown work (Allen, 2011). Bakhtin (1986) proposes that (spoken and written) texts are filled with the echoes of previous speakers/writers and any utterance can only be fully understood against the background of other utterances. For example, the concept *dialogism* describes how the meaning of passages in literature do not exist *in vacuo* but are inextricably in dialogue with other works (Dostoyevsky is dialoguing with Job, for example). These literary echoes, or intertextual connections, imbue texts with dialogic overtones: "An utterance is a link in the chain of speech communication, and it cannot be broken off from the preceding links that determine it both from within and without" (Bakhtin, 1986, p. 94).

Because of these connections, meaning is not just attributable to one particular utterance in isolation but emerges between utterances, texts, and discourses. Fairclough (1992) proposes that the theory of intertextuality should be combined with a theory of power, since the meaning of a text is not infinitely innovative but will be limited by conditions of power, and interpretations of texts that align with discourses of power are more likely. Whereas intertextual analysis attends to the lexico-grammatical features of a text, *interdiscursivity* refers to the connections between texts and discourses. Defined by Fairclough (1992) as "the configuration of discourse conventions that go into [the text's] production" (p. 271), inter-discursive connections reveal how discourses circulating across various physical contexts and layers of discursive activity get reified in policy documents and the media.

Media Discourse

One focus in this chapter is media and, in particular, mainstream online and print publications. Media play an important role in our social and cultural lives, and they are central in perpetuating commonsense notions because of their ability to speak for the masses and/or speak from a supposed neutral stance (Fairclough, 1995; Matheson, 2005; Talbot, 2007). Media can reflect, engender, and normal-ize ideologies about language and language users that, in turn, normalize domi-nant and potentially marginalizing discourses. According to Fairclough (1992), mass media are imbued with hidden power because whole populations are exposed to relatively homogeneous output, which does not include the type of negotiation found in face-to-face interaction. Media discourse is hegemonic if it normalizes dominant or mainstream ways of thinking (and obfuscates alternative accounts) while concomitantly positioning the journalist as a neutral narrator. Yet, Fairclough also asserts that even though the conversation is one-sided, there can be discursive negotiation between the media reader/listener and the "ideal subject" for whom the broadcast or article is written. In other words, a real-life reader might not identify with the assumptions or conclusions the ideal subject (or consumer of media) was meant to take away.

Part of this power emerges from the media's ability to project neutrality or objectivity (however that's interpreted) and, as a consequence, to claim validity. In media discourse, a single article or television report is not as significant as the cumulative effect of presenting information in a particular way over and over. Herman & Chomsky (1988) use the phrase "manufacturing consent" to describe how the media cumulatively promote mainstream interpretations of events and topics that do not necessarily correspond with reality: "Messages…that do not comport with the ideology or interest of gatekeepers and other powerful parties that influence the filtering process [in the media] are at a disadvantage" (Herman & Chomsky, 1988, p. 31). For example, Rickford (1999) describes how media outlets eschewed linguists' reports (including his own) about African American Language (AAL) during the Ebonics debate in the United States in favor of more mainstream or entertaining commentators who did not necessarily understand the history, structure, and linguistics of AAL. After the Oakland School Board crafted a resolution in 1996 that recognized its AAL-speaking students, Rickford notes how the debate that followed was mostly controlled by those who were not experts. The media, he argues, created the impression of (or manufactured) a consensus about AAL that reflected mainstream interpretations and not linguistic findings.

The media landscape has become increasingly diverse, with readers and viewers accessing their preferred outlets from more diverse online and print formats, and media can also challenge dominant and popular ideas about language and disseminate non-mainstream ideas. For example, alternative media, some of which are widely heard (e.g., satellite radio stations), read (e.g., alternative weekly periodicals and web-based news), and seen (e.g., social networking services), often promote *non*-mainstream ideas. Furthermore, the increasing political polarization in the United States aligns with television media that cater to particular political ideologies and are not focused on factual objectivity. Nevertheless, although the analysis in this chapter relies on multiple data sources, we focus primarily on mainstream media outlets that are perceived to be more objective (49 publications). Based on this analysis, we organize the discussion around three major themes: (1) pith, "sciencey" discourse, and hyperbole; (2) pathologization; and (3) parental training.

Pith, Sciencey Discourse, and Hyperbole

Pith, as a technique of concisely portraying the essence of a topic, is important in newspaper articles and helps define the genre, in which long sentences, long words, verbosity, and technical jargon are discouraged (Yopp & McAdams, 1999). Therefore, newspaper articles are not good venues for communicating the complexities and nuances of a research debate. In the spirit of leveraging pith to make ideas easily digestible, language gap research findings are reported on as accepted and monolithic truth and, when divergent findings and arguments that conflict with dominant language gap discourse are reported, they are found at the end of the article. Three features help define pith in media accounts of the language gap: the use of eye-catching numbers as hooks, sciencey discourse, and hyperbole.

One important hook is the use of *leads*, which are important rhetorical devices in newspaper articles for piquing the readers' interest, often in the first line. Leads should be provocative and perhaps startling, and are intended to capture the attention and interest of the news media and audience: "It is the bait to hook the reader" (Yopp & McAdams, 1999, p. 37). There are a few ways this happens in language gap articles – the first is through eye-catching numbers, the most common choice being the 30-million-word gap reported by Hart and Risley:

- A child from a low-income family hears an average of eight million fewer words per year than a child from a wealthier family. That's more than 30 million fewer words by the time the child turns four. (Newman & Kratochwill, 2012)

Another common hook involves personalizing the data with humanizing anecdotes through what are called *affective leads*, which encourage readers to relate to big abstract social problems on a personal or emotional level. For example:

- When 17-month old Deisy Ixcuna-Gonzales takes a bath, her mother talks to her. When Deisy eats breakfast, her mother talks to her. They play, they talk. They eat, they talk. (Sangha, 2014)

The use of this affective lead replaces the actual person, Deisy, with a characterization to which readers presumably relate. We are meant to identify with Deisy, or perhaps her mother. The assumption within this description is that constant talking during all activities – a communicative activity that is not common or natural in most speech communities – is beneficial to Deisy's linguistic development. Deisy Ixcuna-Gonzales is, in fact, a frequent character in media reports on the language gap, showing up in multiple articles about the Providence Talk Initiative.

Another way nuance and complexity are avoided is by replacing the details of complex debates with what we refer to as *sciencey discourse*. The public's misinterpretation of research findings in the natural and social sciences is notoriously problematic. Whether the issue is climate change (Pope, 2019), pandemics and public health (Rivas, 2020), vaccines (Simon & Fox, 2020), or bilingual education (Lam et al., 2020), many media consumers are resistant to evidence-based claims, which is reinforced by political leaders. For example, in response to the Covid-19 pandemic in 2020, Donald Trump regularly espoused the virtues of a medication that research had not only shown to be ineffective in treating the virus, it had actually been shown to be potentially harmful. He summarized his justification in the following way: "I'm taking it, hydroxychloroquine. Right now, yeah. Couple of weeks ago, I started taking it. Cause I think it's good, I've heard a lot of good stories" (as quoted in Lovelace & Breuninger, 2020). Trump's rationale reveals how people will rely less on evidence and research to make medical decisions than on their own instincts, beliefs, and anecdotes, and when faced with a lack of empirical support for their own beliefs and desires they will choose to ignore the research. This phenomenon is often referred to as *confirmation bias*, and numerous psychological studies demonstrate the power personal belief systems have over the interpretation of research findings (Nickerson, 1998; Taber & Lodge, 2006).

A key element of sciencey discourse is obfuscating debate in favor of decisiveness. For example, beginning a sentence with the utterance, "We know that…" is an assertive speech act that performs what Jan Blommaert (2007) calls scale jumping. To invoke authority, doctors will use "we" when suggesting a treatment, and teachers will use "we" when reprimanding students (e.g., "We wait until break to use the bathroom!"). Using "we" instead of "I" jumps from a lower, local, and present scale to a timeless, more widespread scale. Such statements index a social order. The construction "We know that" positions what follows as an epistemological certainty, with no room for debate. It is a discursive move that represents power and leverages a higher level of relevance, truth, value, etc. to cancel out conflicting claims. And, of course, using the verb "know" suggests that there is no debate. The matter is settled. Both Barack Obama and Hillary Clinton have used this construction to describe language gap research:

- *We know that* right now, during the first three years of life, a child born into a low-income family, hears 30 million fewer words than a child born into a well-off family. (Obama, 2014; also quoted by the U.S. Department of Education, 2015)
- *We know that* children build their vocabulary by listening to and interacting with their parents and caregivers. But millions of American parents, especially those struggling to make ends meet or without strong support networks, end up talking and reading to their babies much less frequently than in more affluent families. (Clinton, 2013)

While Obama and Clinton use "We know that...," journalists are typically more formal, but still choose pith over nuance, leveraging phrases like these in major news outlets:

- It's been accepted wisdom... (Zimmer, 2013 – *The Boston Globe*)
- It is a well-known fact... (Tavernise, 2012 – *The New York Times*)
- It is now well established... (Strauss, 2013 – *The Washington Post*)

Additionally, opaque references to "the science" and "scientists" – especially when not named – have a similar effect, normalizing debatable claims as commonsense facts:

- *Scientists have long known* that before they start kindergarten, children from middle-class or affluent families have heard millions more words than youngsters from low-income families... (CBS, 2014)

These discursive moves invoke a larger community of experts, the power of which is strengthened because it is a nameless, faceless community whose authority is unquestioned and unquestionable. Such pith creates the impression that the findings are solid, the debate decided, and the conclusions final. In the text from CBS above, it would be more accurate to say, "Educational psychologists have long argued that..." but the nebulous use of *scientists* and epistemologically definitive verb *know* imbues the utterance with more power. When conflicting findings *are* presented, they are always placed at the end of an article. For example, one article that begins with the 30 million words hook ends with the declaration that it's actually "not about words" (Rich, 2013).

Another aspect of the sciencey discourse in newspaper articles is a heavy reliance on language gap foundations for their reporting, which creates a unified front that portrays the language gap as a monolithic truth. This, in turn, fuels unsubstantiated claims. For example, in a report published by Too Small to Fail, *Word health: Addressing the word gap as a public health crisis*, Crow & O'Leary (2015) describe the impact of the language gap on the physical well-being of children and communities, which contains references to language gap and poverty research, but includes no medical research that would provide evidence of the connections between language and health. They argue that linguistic differences among families are "predictors of children's development, success in school, and even long-term health consequences" (p. 2). Despite the claim, there are no robust research studies that have demonstrated a causal relationship between language development and health disparities. The report thus offers a syllogistic line of reasoning: (1) individuals in poverty experience a language gap; (2) individuals in poverty face more health-related challenges; (3) therefore, the language gap causes health problems. This line of reasoning demonstrates the *post hoc ergo propter hoc* logical fallacy that plagues language gap discourse.

As demonstrated here, public information available through foundation reports can be tricky to navigate. Since they do not adhere to the same rules as academic articles, citations of specific studies are uncommon and, when present, often come from a member of the foundation (as we discuss below). For example, a LENA Foundation promotional report (LENA, 2020) describes the early education initiative LENA Grow as "a professional development program to help teachers in early childhood classrooms (infant, toddler, and pre-kindergarten) increase interactive talk and thereby accelerate children's brain growth and language development" (para. 1) – yet, the empirical justification for the connections between the acquisition of words and "brain growth" is not established. In another example, a Providence Talks (2015) report claims that "[Providence Talks] supports parents in improving the language environments of their children, at the time when brain development science indicates that language development is most critical" (p. 2). In support of this claim, the document includes a footnote citing Dana Suskind's (2015) book, *Thirty million words*. While Dana Suskind is, indeed, a physician, the results in her book rely primarily on Hart & Risley (1995), anecdotal evidence, and her own instincts about the connections between language development and social class. She is also, notably, a member of the advisory board of Providence Talks.

If the crisis is the language gap, the solution must be filling your child up with words. Hyperbolic images, meant to evoke a sense of crisis, accompany Hart & Risley's 2003 publication "The early catastrophe" in *American Educator*. In this abbreviated piece, Hart and Risley include ominous-looking illustrations to enhance the danger of a word gap, here portrayed as a natural catastrophe like an earthquake, which divides two groups of people (presumably, the rich and the poor) and threatens to swallow them. They also include depictions of a parent and child standing on the edge of the chasm, seemingly looking for a way to avoid falling into the abyss of the word gap (Figures 5.1 and 5.2).

FIGURE 5.1 Hart & Risley's (2003) word gap catastrophe

Conflating natural disasters with linguistic processes like language acquisition is clearly hyperbolic, and rather melodramatic considering the scientific claims being portrayed in the publication. Nonetheless, this sense of crisis has also been perpetuated in media reports, which describe the language gap as a "tragic indictment of modern society" (Mansell, 2010) and simply "horrendous" (Wallace, 2014). An NPR piece describes the tension: "It's hopeless…But is it hopeless?" (Spiegel, 2011). In another *American Educator* article on "Overcoming the language gap," Louisa Moats (2001) dejectedly describes her observations of K–12 children from low-income backgrounds: "I watch the gradual toll of word poverty in those children who are struggling."

Hyperbole is a trope that is intentionally and unabashedly deceptive. It relies on excess and exaggeration, but is typically meant to be recognized as exaggeration, as in the expression, "It's a million degrees outside!" However, hyperbole

FIGURE 5.2 Parent and child trying to avoid falling into the word gap (Hart & Risley, 2003)

can also be ontologically and epistemologically disruptive: "Emphasis is produced through hyperbole...when more is said than the truth warrants...so as to give greater force to suspicion" (Cicero, cited in Ritter, 2012). Newspaper writers use hyperbole to entice their readers and dramatize the potentially mundane; however, if the media are understood as neutral, hyperbole blurs into truth, normalizing radical claims as inescapable reality. Accompanying reports of research with hyperbolic images irresponsibly rely on a pathos rhetorical appeal, which contributes to a sciencey discourse that extends beyond the (to be expected) domain of the media to researcher-generated reports of their own research, in which we expect evidence, not hyperbole.

Pathologization

A common feature of language gap discourse is its reliance on *pathologization*, wherein the language practices of the poor are portrayed as causing health problems. Pathologization is an important discursive tool for justifying and normalizing bigotry, and diagnosing differences as deficits instead of socially constructed phenomena (Annamma et al., 2019). For example, Foucault (1978) argues that an explosion of medical discourse around human sexuality, and a corresponding pathologization of homosexuality, justified the bigotry of the state. The medicine of sex, disguised in a discourse of science (a sciencey discourse, if you will), was neither medical nor scientific, but served the medical and juridical control of the body. By shaping the discourse, the "truth" was formed.

Among other examples, Goldberg (1998) argues that new forms of segregation in U.S. society rely on the argument that Black cultural pathology, not racism, is to blame for economic disparities. Similarly, Durrheim & Dixon (2000) reveal that while biological theories of race have been discredited, new forms of cultural racism pathologize racial groups in terms of cultural tendencies, which are an impediment to success in South African society. Through anthropological universals, and what they call "lay ontologies," racism is rendered universally necessary and inevitable. Finally, Saas & Hall (2016) reveal how the political discourse of politicians who advocate for war pathologizes dissent by depicting it as representative of some "nefarious psycho-moral imbalance": i.e., disaffection with war is a kind of "photo-pathogenic disorder, a visually transmitted disease of the American psyche" (p. 181).

Pathologization within language gap discourse relies on opaque and/or undocumented connections between language development and the brain, which never incorporates research from psycholinguistics. Children are portrayed as suffering from not only language deficiencies, but also cognitive deficiencies, which lead to health consequences. For example, in support of language gap initiatives and President Obama's Early Learning Initiative, a U.S. Department of Education publication states:

> It's important to note that talking to one's baby doesn't just promote language development. It promotes brain development more broadly. Every time a parent or caregiver has a positive, engaging verbal interaction with a baby – whether it's talking, singing, or reading – neural connections of all kinds are strengthened within the baby's rapidly growing brain.
>
> *(Shankar, 2014)*

Claims about the connections between language and brain development and "neural connections" are not justified with research findings in foundation reports, because such claims are not supported by research findings. Media reports then help normalize these claims, proclaiming for example, that the "Health consequences can be dire and the benefits of eliminating [the word gap] immense" (Deruy, 2015), and, "Language is the nutrition for a developing brain" (NPR Staff, 2015).

As mentioned above, reports like Crow & O'Leary's (2015) on "Word health" argue that "The lack of words in a child's life amounts to both a public education and public health concern" (p. 6), which necessitates, as an article in *The New Yorker* points out, "The talking cure" (Talbot, 2015). Moreover, another Too Small to Fail publication echoes the language gap as a health crisis via a food deprivation metaphor as a call to action:

> When a child is deprived of food, there is public outrage. And this is because child hunger is correctly identified as a moral and economic issue that moves people to action. We believe that the poverty of vocabulary should be discussed with the same passion as child hunger.
>
> *(Clinton Foundation, n.d., p. 11)*

Parents are thus portrayed as not only denying their children valuable linguistic input but, simultaneously, denying them cognitive nutrition.

Framing the language gap as a public health crisis is the subject of an article published in *The Atlantic*, in which Deruy (2015) covers the Georgia-based initiative Talk With Me Baby, a program designed, as she reports, "to fill the massive 30 million-word gap". It incorporates many of the rhetorical devices discussed in this chapter. First, it begins with an "affective lead" involving a 2-year-old child: "Airon Pate is bouncing off the walls...chattering the entire time. The constant babble exhausts [his mother], 25, but thrills the clinic nutritionist" Deruy (2015). It also utilizes sciencey discourse with opaque references to "the research" in order to justify the argument that "the single best predictor of a child's academic success is not parental education or socioeconomic status, but rather the quality and quantity of the words that a baby hears during his or her first three years." To support these claims, experts are quoted:

> While the word gap might sound like an education problem, the health consequences can be dire—and the benefits of eliminating it can be immense. Public-health officials in Georgia recognize this. "This is pure biology," Brenda Fitzgerald, Georgia's Health Commissioner and the woman in charge of state public-health programs, said during an interview at her Atlanta office. "Which is why it's a public-health initiative.
>
> *Deruy (2015, para. 7–8)*

After her term as Georgia's Health Commissioner, Fitzgerald was appointed by Donald Trump to be the director of the Centers for Disease Control and Prevention for a very brief period, during which time it was exposed that she was invested in cancer detection and health information technology. Describing the word gap as "pure biology" explicitly justifies the eugenic claims only hinted at in other areas of language gap discourse. Elsewhere, Deruy's piece relies on logical fallacies:

> Adults who were *good students and earned a college degree* have longer life expectancies. They are at a *lower risk* for hypertension, depression, and sleep problems. They are less likely to be smokers and to be obese. "There is no way we can separate health and education," said Jennifer Stapel-Wax, director of infant and toddler clinical research operations at the Marcus Autism Center in Atlanta, and the self-described "chief cheerleader" for the effort.
>
> *(para. 9–10, emphasis in original)*

Here, Deruy relies on a syllogistic argument that incorporates a similar logical fallacy as discussed above: (1) adults who had educational success experience fewer health problems; (2) children with more words do better in school; therefore (3) children who hear fewer words now will suffer health consequences later.

Absent from this syllogistic argument are other factors that impact educational attainment and the overall process of schooling, that tend to adversely impact students from linguistically diverse backgrounds. Instead, this argument portrays the home language environment (i.e., how parents talk) as pathological. Additionally, an instructional flyer from Talk With Me Baby (2016) proclaims "Language nutrition is free!" and entreats parents to "feed their baby's brain with a steady diet of words." In one sidebar section of text, they urge parents, "Feed Your Baby's Brain," under which they provide the following guidance:

- All parents want the best for their baby. And we know healthy food helps grow a healthy baby. But to grow a healthy brain, babies need more. Babies need lots of loving words. (p. 1)

They even provide a (trademarked) statement on "Language nutrition: A public health and education imperative" (Talk With Me Baby, n.d.). The implication is that not heeding the advice of language gap institutions means parents do not want the best for their babies and will therefore deprive them of necessary linguistic nutrition, which in turn will lead to health problems. The message is: If you do not speak to your children in the correct way, you are literally making them sick.

Parental Training: Talking = Teaching

A key aspect of language gap discourse is how it taps into a culture of poverty discourse (Ladson-Billings, 2017), whereby individual character traits – in this case language practices – are blamed for educational inequities, while structural inequalities in schools and society are ignored. Parents are patronizingly told that they do not speak to their children in the correct way, but they can improve if they agree to take part in one of the language gap programs. The salvation of poor parents is contrasted with the already-saved middle- and upper-class parent. Characterized simply as "the talkative mom" in a 2013 article in *The Washington Post* (Strauss, 2013), for example, the middle-class parent is portrayed as proceeding in a near constant mode of annotation, reading poetry to their children *in utero*, describing fruit at the supermarket, and pointing out the shape of a stop sign. The converse, of course, and the implication, is that because poor children do not exist in continuous receipt of dictation, they are deprived by their parents who lack the appropriate ambition to talk to their children in the correct way. Low-income parents influenced by the wrong cultural norms therefore require interventions, which include a focus on sociolinguistic norms that reflect White middle-class speech communities and their communicative practices. Preferred communicative activities, which are *a priori* assumed to be superior, include eye contact, constant quizzing, parental narration of their own activities, peppering the children with questions, and the use of display questions, which, as Blum (in Avineri et al., 2015) argues, is an unnatural speech act for many cultures.

These claims are reinforced in foundation documents, which contend that "Highly educated mothers spend more time with children, read to them more, and use more complex language when speaking with their children as compared to less educated mothers" (Crow & O'Leary, 2015, p. 6). Foundation "tip sheets" published by Too Small to Fail, Talk With Me Baby, and the U.S. Department of Education suggest ditching the baby talk, asking questions that require a choice, singing, and making eye contact. More explicit instructions include:

- A stop sign, a traffic light, or a tree might seem boring to you, but it's a whole new world to your child, so talk to them about it! (Too Small to Fail, n.d.).
- Let's turn 'wash time' into 'talk time'! Laundromats aren't just for washing clothes! (Talking is Teaching, 2016)
- Move to the child's level and make eye contact (U.S. Department of Education, n.d.)
- Use eye contact, make facial expressions, smile, and gesture (Talk With Me Baby, 2016)

Such suggestions are repeated in the media, which portray every moment of the day as an opportunity to fill your children with words. For example, "Bath time could be a teachable moment" (NPR Staff, 2013). Other suggestions are deeply strange, including the following, which is repeated across media outlets, even though the source is unclear: "Instead of turning on music while fixing lunch, talk about the bowl of fruit on the table!" (Associated Press, 2019). Or, this suggestion published by *CNN Health*, which is perhaps more to the point: "Talk to your baby like you talk to your dog" (Strauss, 2018).

As parents, we would argue that bath time with our babies is often a stressful moment, another in a series of tasks that occupy nearly every waking hour of the parents' day. Still, a moment of solace is possible when everyone is quiet. In language gap discourse, parents are teachers and talking is instruction, and every hour of the day is an opportunity to teach. Furthermore, while already struggling and marginalized poorer parents are targeted, economically privileged parents need no interventions because they are already ambitious: "Ambitious parents who are already reading poetry and playing Mozart to their children in utero" (Rich, 2014, para. 5). "The ambitious parent is always talking...the child exists in continuous receipt of dictation" (Bellafante, 2012).

Conclusion: The Language Gap Echo Chamber

There is a tendency in the media to frame the language gap research findings as monolithic, even in publication outlets that strive to be more objective (e.g., González, 2015; Lahey, 2014). That said, the recent publication of Sperry et al.'s research (2019a,b) (see Chapter 3) has resulted in a spike in coverage that is more nuanced. At one end of the spectrum, Kamenetz's (2018) NPR article "Let's stop talking about the 30 million word gap" first outlines Hart and Risley's original study, then points to Gilkerson et al.'s (2017) "4 million" word finding. She then follows by highlighting Sperry et al.'s work, as well as Adair et al.'s (2017) study on the ideological impact of the language gap on educators. On the other end, Pondiscio's (2019) article "Don't dismiss that 30-million word gap quite so fast" mentions Sperry's work, as well as articles like Kamenetz's, but falls back on quotes from language gap researchers that frame the "gap" as urgent and meriting attention. Other media publications that attempt to maintain an objective description of both sides of the debate and provide links to a variety of perspectives include McKenna (2018) and Rothschild (2016).

Although there may be an increase in media that cover findings refuting the language gap, the majority of media simply repeat Hart and Risley's numbers *ad infinitum*, and stay trapped in the echo chamber that reinforces debatable research findings as monolithic truths about the connections between language, social class, educational achievement, and health. By burying conflicting accounts, emphasizing a sense of crisis, pathologizing non-middle-class sociolinguistic norms, and through sheer repetition, language gap discourse manufactures consent (Herman & Chomsky, 1988). Lower-income parents, who already face formidable obstacles (racism, poverty, nativism, actual health care issues), are patronizingly told that talking to their kids more is an educational and economic panacea.

Gramsci (1971) argues that hegemonic power structures are disguised through a process of social conformism and normalization. By blaming the poor for educational and health disparities, and obfuscating the role of structural inequities in schools and society, language gap discourse taps into the culture of poverty discourse. Media reports about the language gap and foundation documents reinforce popular ideologies about language, education, and social class, which in turn reinforce economic and educational inequality as the natural order of things. As Dana Suskind argues, "It doesn't happen with one intervention…It happens when an idea takes hold in a population" (quoted in NPR Staff, 2015). Despite Suskind's concerns, we argue that the idea has already "taken hold."

While we agree that minoritized language users should be exposed to academic language and different language varieties, home language varieties and skills should also be a part of schooling and not targeted as deficits. By ignoring cultural and linguistic diversity, language gap adherents miss the opportunity to help children develop metalinguistic and critical language awareness, value their home language skills, and develop academic registers in multiple languages and dialects. Helping children understand the value of different language proficiencies across multiple contexts should be the goal – without solely prioritizing the legitimacy of the language forms promoted in school. Demonstrating communicative competence, for example, is not simply a matter of using dictionary words, but sometimes, as Hymes (1972) argues, it's important to be appropriately *ungrammatical*. Communicative competence requires that we alter our register, dialect, speech acts, etc. to the speech situation in question. Language gap research does not capture, and foundation and media reports do not celebrate what other research has shown: word play, metaphor, and complex narrative events all demonstrate linguistic complexity.

When someone writes a newspaper article about the language gap, no matter where they tap in – through foundations, research, or particular scholars – they're going to get caught in an echo chamber. When looking for quotes, writers will be referred to other language gap research by other language gap scholars and/or by foundation members, which invariably supports the goals of the foundations. As displayed in Figure 5.3, language gap researchers, who are often members of – or funded by – language gap organizations, develop the programs. Language gap researchers secure funding from language gap organizations, publish their findings, which inform the organizations' programs, and then get further funding from the same organization. At every stage, media reports are generated that highlight language gap research and programs, which validate the language gap research and foundation funding, not to mention broader social support for further language gap research and programs – and the cycle continues.

The intertextual and interdisursive connections within the echo chamber that promote language deficit discourses – within an ideological-discursive formation (Fairclough, 2010) – privilege middle- and upper-class English language varieties and their speakers who do not endure economic and linguistic marginalization. Economically disadvantaged parents are thus "scapegoats" in the debate, in which non-dominant ideas are silenced in a language gap discourse that normalizes educational inequity for economically disadvantaged children.

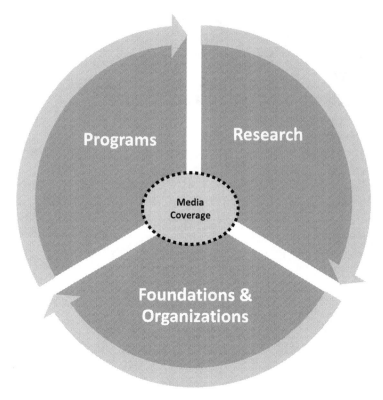

FIGURE 5.3 The language gap echo chamber

Low-income families are encouraged to "misrecognize" the inherent value of their communication abilities by seeing themselves as the problem (Bourdieu, 1977), a process that obfuscates broader social processes that engender economic and educational (dis)advantages. Thus, language gap discourse and neoliberal logic combine to normalize increased marginalization of the already marginalized.

Portraying their solution as an educational panacea – i.e. that parents should fill their children up with words – language gap researchers cite verbal deficits as the best predictor for eventual educational achievement, and politicians and educational organizations appropriate these arguments, despite a history of educational research documenting a diversity of social and sociolinguistic factors that impact educational opportunity for minoritized students. Thus, what is considered "normal" – i.e., White middle-class linguistic and sociolinguistic norms – is based on the "prescriptive character of the norm," which positions minoritized language varieties as abnormal (Foucault, 2007, p. 57) and pathologizes the sociolinguistic and language socialization processes that incorporate them (Foucault, 1978). In this chapter, we have examined how linguistic deficit discourses emerge from the language gap literature, permeate language gap foundations in the U.S., and find their way into the media; we encourage others to explore these same connections and think critically about how the language gap is portrayed in the public sphere.

References

Adair, J. K., Colegrove, K. S. S., & McManus, M. E. (2017). How the word gap argument negatively impacts young children of Latinx immigrants' conceptualizations of learning. *Harvard Educational Review*, 87(3), 309–334.

Allen, G. (2011). *Intertextuality*. Routledge.

American Academy of Pediatrics. (2014). Literacy promotion: An essential component of primary care pediatric practice (Policy statement). *Pediatrics*, 34(2), 404–409. http://pediatrics.aappublications.org/content/pediatrics/134/2/404.full.pdf

Annamma, S. A., Anyon, Y., Joseph, N. M., Farrar, J., Greer, E., Downing, B., & Simmons, J. (2019). Black girls and school discipline: The complexities of being overrepresented and understudied. *Urban Education*, 54(2), 211–242.

Associated Press. (2014). How to talk to babies and toddlers to help them develop language skills. *The Oregonian* (updated January 10, 2019). https://www.oregonlive.com/kiddo/2014/02/tips_for_talking_to_babies_and.html

Association for Library Service to Children. (2020). Babies need words every day: Talk, read, sing, play. http://www.ala.org/alsc/babiesneedwords

Avineri, N., Johnson, E. J., Brice-Heath, S., McCarty, T., Ochs, E., Kremer-Sadlik, T., Blum, S., Zentella, A. C., Rosa, J., Flores, N., Alim, H. S., & Paris, D. (2015). Invited forum: Bridging the "language gap." *Journal of Linguistic Anthropology*, 25(1), 66–86.

Bakhtin, M. M. (1986). *Speech genres and other late essays*. University of Texas Press.

Bellafante, G. (2012). Before a test, a poverty of words. *The New York Times*, October 5. http://www.nytimes.com/2012/10/07/nyregion/for-poor-schoolchildren-a-poverty-of-words.html

Blommaert, J. (2001). Context is/as critique. *Critique of Anthropology*, 21(1), 13–32.

Blommaert, J. (2007). Sociolinguistic scales. *Intercultural Pragmatics*, 4(1), 1–20.

Bourdieu, P. (1977). *Outline of a theory of practice*. Cambridge University Press.

CBS. (2014). Speaking to babies in long sentences boosts language development. *CBS News*, February 14. http://www.cbsnews.com/news/speaking-to-babies-in-long-sentences-boosts-language-development/

Clinton, H. (2013). Closing the 'word gap.'https://www.clintonfoundation.org/blog/2013/10/03/closing-word-gap

Clinton Foundation. (n.d.). Preparing America's children for success in the 21st century: Too small to fail. https://www.clintonfoundation.org/files/2s2f_framingreport_v2r3.pdf

Crow, S., & O'Leary, A. (2015). *Word health: Addressing the word gap as a public health crisis.* Next Generation and Too Small to Fail

Deruy, E. (2015). Why boosting poor children's vocabulary is important for public health. *The Atlantic*, September 7. http://www.theatlantic.com/education/archive/2015/09/georgias-plan-to-close-the-30-million-word-gap-for-kids/403903/

Durrheim, K., & Dixon, J. (2000). Theories of culture in racist discourse. *Race and Society*, 3(2), 93–109.

Fairclough, N. (1992). Intertextuality in critical discourse analysis. *Linguistics and Education*, 4, 269–293.

Fairclough, N. (1995). *Media discourse*. Bloomsbury.

Fairclough, N. (2010). *Critical discourse analysis: The critical study of language*. Routledge.

Fairclough, N. (2015). *Language and power*. Routledge.

Foucault, M. (1978). *The history of sexuality*. Random House.

Foucault, M. (2007). *Security, territory, population: Lectures at the Collège de France 1977–1978*. Palgrave.

Fowler, R., Hodge, B., Kress, G., & Trew, T. (1979). *Language and social control*. Routledge.

Gilkerson, J., Richards, J. A., Warren, S. F., Montgomery, J. K., Greenwood, C. R., Oller, D. K., Hansen, J. H. L., & Paul, T. D. (2017). Mapping the early language environment using all-day recordings and automated analysis. *American Journal of Speech-Language Pathology*, 26(2), 248–265.

Goldberg, D. T. (1998). The new segregation. *Race and Society*, 1(1), 15–32.

González, C. (2015). 30-million 'word gap' divides rich and poor kids. *The Atlantic*, June 15. https://www.theatlantic.com/politics/archive/2015/06/30-million-word-gap-divides-rich-and-poor-kids/432135/

Gramsci, A. (1971). *Selections from the prison notebooks of Antonio Gramsci*. Q. Hoare & G. N. Smith (Eds.). International Publishers.

Halliday, M. A. K. (1978). *Language as social semiotic: The social interpretation of language and meaning*. Edward Arnold.

Hart, B., & Risley, T. (1995). *Meaningful differences in the everyday experiences of young American children*. Brookes Publishing.

Hart, B., & Risley, T. (2003). The early catastrophe. *American Educator*, 27(4), 6–9.

Herman, E. S., & Chomsky, N. (1988). *Manufacturing consent: The political economy of the mass media*. Pantheon Books.

Hult, F. M., & Johnson, D. C. (Eds.) (2015). *Research methods in language policy and planning: A practical guide*. Wiley-Blackwell.

Hymes, D. (1972). On communicative competence. In J. B. Pride & J. Holmes (Eds.), *Sociolinguistics: Selected readings*. (pp. 269–293). Penguin.

Johnson, D.C. (2016). Intertextuality and language policy. In F. M. Hult & D. C. Johnson (Eds.), *Research methods in language policy and planning: A practical guide*. Wiley-Blackwell.

Johnson, D. C., Johnson, E. J., & Hetrick, D. (2020). Normalization of language deficit ideologies for a new generation of minoritized U.S. youth. *Social Semiotics*, 30(4), doi:10.1080/10350330.2020.1766210

Kamenetz, A. (2018). Let's stop talking about the '30 million word gap'." *NPR*, June 1. https://www.npr.org/sections/ed/2018/06/01/615188051/lets-stop-talking-about-the-30-million-word-gap

Kristeva, J. (1986). Word, dialogue, and novel. In T. Moi (Ed.), *The Kristeva reader* (pp. 34–61). Basil Blackwell.

Krzyżanowski, M. (2020). Normalization and the discursive construction of "new" norms and "new" normality: Discourse in the paradoxes of populism and neoliberalism. *Social Semiotics*, 30(4), 431–448. doi:10.1080/10350330.2020.1766193

Ladson-Billings, G. (2017). "Makes me wanna holler": Refuting the "culture of poverty" discourse in urban schooling. *American Academy of Political and Social Science*, 673, 80–90.

Lahey, J. (2014). Poor kids and the 'word gap.' *The Atlantic*, October 16. http://www.theatlantic.com/education/archive/2014/10/american-kids-are-starving-for-words/381552/

Lam, K., Lam, K., & Richards, E. (2020). More US schools teach in English and Spanish, but not enough to help Latino kids. *USA Today*, May 24. https://www.usatoday.com/

in-depth/news/education/2020/01/06/english-language-learners-benefit-from-dual-language-immersion-bilingual-education/4058632002/

LENA (2020). *LENA Grow: Transform interactions in child care through experiential professional development.* https://cdn2.hubspot.net/hubfs/3975639/08.%20LENA%20Grow/4.%20LENA_Grow_Proposal.pdf

Lovelace, B. & Breuninger, K. (2020). Trump says he takes hydroxychloroquine to prevent coronavirus infection even though it's an unproven treatment. *CNBC*, May 18. https://www.cnbc.com/2020/05/18/trump-says-he-takes-hydroxychloroquine-to-prevent-coronavirus-infection.html

Matheson, D. (2005). *Media discourses: Analysing media texts.* Open University Press.

Mansell, W. (2010). Poor children a year behind in language skills. *The Guardian*, February 15. https://www.theguardian.com/education/2010/feb/15/poor-children-behind-sutton-trust

McKenna, L. (2018). The long, contentious history of the 'word gap' study. *The Atlantic*, June 15. https://www.theatlantic.com/education/archive/2018/06/the-long-contentious-history-of-the-word-gap-study/562850/

Moats. L. (2001). Overcoming the language gap. *American Educator.* https://www.aft.org/periodical/american-educator/summer-2001/overcoming-language-gap-0

Newman, J. & Kratochwill, L. (2012). Falling behind before kindergarten: The 30 million word gap. *WBEZ*, June 15. https://www.wbez.org/shows/wbez-news/falling-behind-before-kindergarten-the-30-million-word-gap/b2d9fc53-4a20-4d63-8d40-93499fee0ffb

Nickerson, R. S. (1998). Confirmation bias: A ubiquitous phenomenon in many guises. *Review of General Psychology*, 2(2), 175–220.

NPR Staff. (2013). Closing the 'word gap' between rich and poor. *NPR*, December 29. http://www.npr.org/2013/12/29/257922222/closing-the-word-gap-between-rich-and-poor

NPR Staff. (2015). Simple number, complex impact. How many words has a child heard? *NPR*, December 5. https://www.npr.org/2015/12/05/458501823/simple-number-complex-impact-how-many-words-has-a-child-heard

Obama, B. (2014). Empowering our children by bridging the word gap. https://www.youtube.com/watch?v=NhC3n7oUm9U#action=share

Pondiscio, R. (2019). Don't dismiss that 30 million-word gap quite so fast. *EducationNext*, June 6. https://www.educationnext.org/dont-dismiss-30-million-word-gap-quite-fast/

Pope, C. (2019). Climate change became a burning issue in the past decade, but also an opportunity. *NBC News*, December 28. https://www.nbcnews.com/think/opinion/climate-change-became-burning-issue-past-decade-also-opportunity-ncna1108101

Providence Talks. (2015). Pilot findings & next steps. http://www.providencetalks.org/wp-content/uploads/2015/10/Providence-Talks-Pilot-Findings-Next-Steps.pdf

Rich, M. (2014). Pediatrics group to recommend reading aloud to children from birth. *The New York Times*, June 24. http://www.nytimes.com/2014/06/24/us/pediatrics-group-to-recommend-reading-aloud-to-children-from-birth.html?_r=0

Rickford, J. R. (1999). *African American vernacular English: Features, evolution, educational implications.* Blackwell.

Ritter, J. R. (2012). Recovering hyperbole: Rethinking the limits of rhetoric for an age of excess. *Philosophy & Rhetoric*, 45(4), 406–428.

Rivas, K. (2020). Coronavirus update: States rolling back, delaying reopenings amid pandemic. *Fox News*, July 1. https://www.foxnews.com/health/coronavirus-update-these-states-rolled-back-or-paused-reopenings-amid-pandemic

Rothschild, A. (2016). Beyond the word gap: Are efforts to boost kids' vocabularies before kindergarten missing the mark? *The Atlantic*, April 22. https://www.theatlantic.com/education/archive/2016/04/beyond-the-word-gap/479448/

Rumsey, A. (1990). Wording, meaning, and linguistic ideology. *American Anthropologist*, 92(2), 346–361.

Ryan, E. B., Giles, H., & Sebastian, R. J. (1982). An integrative perspective for the study of attitudes toward language variation. In E. B. Ryan & H. Giles (Eds.), *Attitudes towards language variation: Social and applied contexts* (1–19). Edward Arnold.

Sangha, S. (2014). The serious business of baby talk: How one pilot program aims to improve the lives of low-income kids. *Fox News Latino*, May 5. http://latino.foxnews.com/latino/lifestyle/2014/05/05/serious-business-baby-talk-how-one-pilot-program-aims-to-improve-lives-low/

Saas, W. O., & Hall, R. (2016). Restive peace: Body bags, casket flags, and the pathologization of dissent. *Rhetoric and Public Affairs*, 19(2), 177–208.

Shankar, M. (2014). Empowering our children by bridging the word gap. *The White House*, June 25. https://www.whitehouse.gov/blog/2014/06/25/empowering-our-children-bridging-word-gap

Simon, M., & Fox, M. (2020). Pfizer and BioNTech begin large-scale trial of coronavirus vaccine in the United States. *CNN Health*, July 28. https://www.cnn.com/2020/07/28/health/pfizer-coronavirus-vaccine-trial-begins-biontech/index.html

Sperry, D. E., Sperry, L. L., & Miller, P. J. (2019a). Reexamining the verbal environments of children from different socioeconomic backgrounds. *Child Development*, 90(4), 1303–1318.

Spiegel, A. (2011). Closing the achievement gap with baby talk. *National Public Radio*, January 10. http://www.npr.org/2011/01/10/132740565/closing-the-achievement-gap-with-baby-talk

Strauss, E. (2018). Talk to your baby like you talk to your dog. *CNN Health*, November 7. https://www.cnn.com/2018/11/07/health/baby-talk-language-development-parenting-strauss/index.html

Strauss, V. (2013). The 'early language gap' is about more than word. *The Washington Post*, November 1. https://www.washingtonpost.com/news/answer-sheet/wp/2013/11/01/the-early-language-gap-is-about-more-than-words/

Suskind, D. (2015). *Thirty million words: Building a child's brain: tune in, talk more, take turns.* Dutton.

Taber, C. S., & Lodge, M. (2006). Motivated skepticism in the evaluation of political beliefs. *American Journal of Political Science*, 50(3), 755–769.

Talbot, M. (2007). *Media discourse.* Edinburgh University Press.

Talbot, M. (2015). The talking cure. *The New Yorker*, January 5. http://www.newyorker.com/magazine/2015/01/12/talking-cure

Talk With Me Baby. (n.d.). Language nutrition: A public health and education imperative. http://www.talkwithmebaby.org/language_nutrition#:~:text=Language%20Nutrition%E2%84%A2%20%E2%80%93%20A%20Public,is%20critical%20to%20brain%20development

Talk With Me Baby. (2016). Learn the skills. https://d3n8a8pro7vhmx.cloudfront.net/twmb/pages/70/attachments/original/1462224017/LearntheSkills.pdf?1462224017

Talking Is Teaching. (2016). Let's turn 'wash time' into 'talk time'!https://talkingisteaching.org/resources/laundry-tipsheet

Tavernise, S. (2012). Education gap grows between rich and poor, studies say. *The New York Times*, October 2. http://www.nytimes.com/2012/02/10/education/education-gap-grows-between-rich-and-poor-studies-show.html

Too Small to Fail (n.d.). *Building young brains through talking, reading, and singing.* http://toosmall.org/community/body/Research-and-Tips.pdf

U.S. Department of Education. (n.d.). *Talk, read, and sing together every day: Tip sheets for families, caregivers, and early learning educators.* http://www.ed.gov/early-learning/talk-read-sing

U.S. Department of Education. (2015). Bridging the word gap. White House Initiative on Educational Excellence for Hispanics. https://sites.ed.gov/hispanic-initiative/2015/05/bridging-the-word-gap/

U.S. Department of Health and Human Services. (2017). Bridging the word gap. Child Health & Development. https://www.acf.hhs.gov/ecd/child-health-development/bridging-the-word-gap

Wallace, K. (2014). Parents should read aloud to infants every day, pediatricians say. *CNN,* June 25. http://www.cnn.com/2014/06/25/living/doctors-read-aloud-to-infants-parents/index.html

Wodak, R. (1996). *Disorders of discourse.* Longman.

Woolard, K. A. & Schieffelin, B. B. (1994). Language ideology. *Annual Review of Anthropology,* 23, 55–82.

Yopp, J. J., McAdams, K. C. (1999). *Reaching audiences: A guide to media writing.* Allyn and Bacon.

Zimmer, B. (2013). Providence's $5 million plan to shrink the 'word gap'. *The Boston Globe,* March 23. https://www.bostonglobe.com/ideas/2013/03/23/providence-million-plan-shrink-word-gap/zwVX3JKvmsZChHVPimovbN/story.html

6

THE LANGUAGE GAP AND EDUCATION

David Cassels Johnson and Eric J. Johnson

In the previous chapters, we analyzed how deficit discourses are engendered by language gap research, promoted by language gap organizations, and recontextualized in public policy and the media. This chapter addresses U.S. education. We begin with a challenging question: How do we move away from describing diverse linguistic backgrounds and abilities in terms of deficits while simultaneously emphasizing the fundamental systemic inequities that continue to impact the educational and economic opportunities for students who are already marginalized? This is one of the central challenges for the fields of educational linguistics, sociolinguistics, and anthropology, which have produced many contextualized examples of successful approaches for working with diverse students, families, and their schools.

Normalizing Linguistic Deficits and Blaming Parents

Instead of championing specific language skills, features, varieties, and types of knowledge as inherently superior, research in Sociolinguistics and Linguistic Anthropology attempts to understand how linguistic and cultural patterns are inherently complex and contextually dependent. Zentella's (2005) description of language socialization patterns in linguistically diverse contexts reveals that different cultural groups orient their children to group norms in varied ways. She reminds us that children become speakers of their language by using language to become competent members of their speech communities. In other words, novice members of a speech community are socialized to, and through, language (Ochs & Schieffelin, 2014). For example, whereas some groups might see a child who asks multiple questions and demands expanded answers as smart/intellectual, other groups might see the same child as rude and disrespectful. How we use language, learn about the world around us, and develop "knowledge" is culturally determined according to the social context and the speech communities in which we are socialized. Furthermore, the types of knowledge that are valued (as well as the contexts that are seen as beneficial for learning) are impacted by societal hierarchies of power. For example, while White middle-class parents in the U.S. often encourage their children to be competent interlocutors, in other cultures child-centered speech is not employed in the same way and children are expected to be bystanders to adult conversation.

The ways families interact at home and within their communities is often very different than the way educators and students interact in classrooms, and kids must learn how to leverage their verbal repertoires to communicate in their communities. The classroom is a unique sociolinguistic context to which kids must acclimate, and this requires socialization into the academic discourse that is reflected and valued in schools. Thus, all students must learn how to "do school" – an activity that is culturally and linguistically specific. For example, in the U.S., young students must learn how to line up to leave the classroom and raise their hands when they want to participate, neither of which are universal activities in all classrooms around the world. As well, all kids are expected to appropriate a culturally specific academic discourse and, while this is a challenge for everyone, the linguistic and sociolinguistic practices that are privileged in schools reflect White middle-class norms and tend to marginalize the linguistic and cultural resources that multilingual and multidialectal individuals bring to the classroom.

To help mitigate these academic challenges, scholars like Heath (2000) and Alim (2005) argue that educators must understand and incorporate their students' linguistic and sociolinguistic practices. Yet, while Heath and Alim argue that schools need to change, language gap organizations and researchers place the onus of responsibility on the parents, and the solution proposed is parental training: Parents do not talk to their children enough, or in the correct way, and they require interventions that will teach them to improve. For example, Wasik & Hindman (2015) encourage adults to engage in "high quality conversations" by essentially replicating classroom discourse patterns: e.g., introducing new vocabulary, applying "wait time" strategies, using open-ended questions, and providing "quality" feedback (pp. 52–53). Additionally, Golinkoff et al. (2019) argue that "we must consider how to 'language-ize' children's homes, day cares, and schools" to overcome academic achievement disparities (p. 990). Such patronizing suggestions, propelled by the notion that school-based language practices are inherently superior, as opposed to (socio)linguistically idiosyncratic, ignore how much these speech acts would not demonstrate communicative competence within the children's speech communities and would, in fact, be interpreted as quite strange and potentially violating sociolinguistic norms of interaction. This is perhaps the most pernicious impact of language gap research – the demonization of parents. Instead of recognizing – or attempting to understand – the variety of ways in which children are socialized into speech communities, language gap proponents insist that low socioeconomic status (SES) parents need to change the way they talk to their children to avoid long-term educational and health problems.

Some researchers have focused on the education of the parents as the problem (e.g., Golinkoff et al., 2019; Hoff, 2013). As Hart & Risley (1995) argue, "The educated parents we observed, themselves the children of educated parents, were transmitting to the next generation an upper-SES culture with its care for politeness" (p. 58). Similarly, Rowe (2008) argues that "Parents who come from more educated and advantaged backgrounds may have greater language skills and more verbal facilities to draw on " (p. 188). Such claims ignore sociolinguistic research demonstrating complex language practices in all communities, regardless of income and level of education (e.g., Labov, 1972). In other cases where anthropological research is dismissed, language gap scholars miss the opportunity to draw on language socialization research to explain how school communication patterns are reproduced by individuals (i.e., teachers and other students) who are successful in academic settings (e.g., Rowe, 2008, p. 187). Instead, being "educated" is associated with an ethno/SES-centric perspective of intelligence and "greater language skills."

The condemnation of parents' language use is often tied to questions about their childrearing abilities. For example, Dana Suskind, founder of the Thirty Million Words initiative, contends that not providing the right amount or type of language will negatively impact a child's "life trajectory" (Suskind et al., 2013, p. 207) and, therefore, interventions are needed to improve the language of parents who have a lower "maternal knowledge of child development" (Leffel & Suskind, 2013, p. 269). Hart and Risley quite explicitly conflate their measures of linguistic sophistication with "measures of parenting," both of which are based on researcher assumptions about what constitutes the best language *and* the best parenting. For example, under "measures of parenting," they include "the extent to which the parent tends to keep the child in visual range" and "the extent to which the parent talks to the child while doing other work" (Hart & Risley, 1992, p. 1098). They suggest utilizing indirect requests, as opposed to directives, which reflects an "upper-SES culture with its care for politeness" (Hart & Risley, 1995, p. 58). There is no justification for why these are good measures of language, let alone good measures of parenting, and there is no consideration of how parenting styles differ across cultures (e.g., Ashdown & Faherty, 2020). Instead, socialization practices that typically reflect White middle-class norms are valorized, not as cultural practices, but as simply superior. Suggested interventions include eye contact, constant quizzing, parental narration of their own activities, peppering the children with questions, and the use of display questions, which, as Blum (in Avineri et al., 2015) argues, is a strange speech act that demonstrates performance for a judging audience.

In her critique of Hart and Risley, Rolstad (2014) puts it this way,

> Rather than asking, *Is there something different about the way these children's language is developing? If there is a difference, is it a developmental problem with cognitive consequences?*, these researchers ask, *What is wrong with the language of these other people's children, and how is it responsible (directly or indirectly) for poverty?*.
>
> (p. 3, emphasis ours)

Language gap discourse normalizes the assumption that there is something wrong with the linguistic practices of poor communities, who are to blame for educational inequality, and perpetuating their own poverty. Relying on the culture of poverty discourse (Ladson-Billings, 2017), such arguments ignore how structural inequalities in society impact educational inequities in schools, both of which perpetuate the marginalization of the poor.

What Else Might Explain Differences in Educational Achievement?

Examinations of how structural inequalities shape U.S. schools have been explored in recent decades (e.g., Delpit, 2006; Kozol, 1991; McCarty, 2005) and there have been widespread calls for pedagogies that are "culturally relevant" (Ladson-Billings, 1995, 2014), "culturally responsive" (Gay, 2010), and "culturally sustaining" (Paris & Alim, 2014, 2017). These intellectual and educational movements push for a change in how minoritized students are engaged in schools, and demand that educators learn about their students' backgrounds and build on their "funds of knowledge" (González et al., 2005) to enhance academic experiences and learning.

Despite the research showing the impact of societal inequalities on education, language gap researchers argue that "language ability in early childhood is the *single best* predictor of school readiness and later school success" (Hirsh-Pasek et al., 2015, p. 1071, emphasis ours), suggesting that parental language interventions are a panacea for educational inequity. These claims are often accompanied by flawed syllogistic and polysyllogistic reasoning that relies on false assumptions to connect home language practices to academic success and cognitive development. For example:

1.   Success in school requires use of particular language varieties and features;
2.   Students who utilize different language varieties and features are often unsuccessful in school;

Therefore,

3.   The language practices in the home are the best predictor of academic success.

While there is plenty of research support for (1) and (2), the conclusion drawn in (3) makes the logical fallacy of *post hoc ergo propter hoc* because it ignores a wealth of other research demonstrating other factors that influence academic success. Beyond language gap studies, which tend to stay stuck in an echo chamber with other language gap research (e.g., Hirsh-Pasek et al., 2015 cite another language gap researcher, Hoff, to validate the claim above), research suggests that there are myriad potential factors affecting disparities in educational achievement, including school segregation, racism, poverty, mental health, exposure to violence, teacher-child ratios, and the educational level of teachers (Becker & Luthar, 2002; Gregory et al., 2010; Lee & Bowen, 2006).

Another line of argumentation is used to blame families for their own economic and educational marginalization:

1. The language practices in low-SES communities lead to educational inequity;
2. Educational inequity leads to poverty;

Therefore,

3. The language practices of low-SES communities perpetuate their own poverty.

This argument taps into the culture of poverty discourse, which blames individuals for their own poverty while ignoring societal inequality. The solution proposed within language gap discourse is not to challenge educators and policymakers to interrogate how linguistic and pedagogical practices in schools privilege some while marginalizing others; the solution is for the already marginalized families to change.

Instead of capturing a cause–effect relationship between communicative practices and educational achievement, language gap research highlights how some kids lack the type of linguistic capital that is preferred in K-12 schools, which includes knowledge of White middle-class language socialization practices and associated language varieties (see Lee & Bowen, 2006). As Rowe argues, parents from middle-class homes provide their children "with practice in the forms of discourse they must come to master in school" (2012: 1764). This claim reflects empirical findings from Heath (1983) and Philips (1983), which have shown how White middle-class families leverage their social training and institutional experience to ensure their children's success. However, the solutions proposed are very different, and we argue that strapping word pedometers to parents and asking them to speak to their children in unnatural ways are not effective approaches for improving educational equity in schools and, in fact, have the opposite impact: re-conceptualizing deficits for a new generation of marginalized youth.

Furthermore, even when students are in the same SES group, racism and school segregation contribute to disparities between Black and White students (Burchinal et al., 2011). For example, while "parental involvement" tends to correspond with educational achievement (Spera, 2005), research shows that White parents accrue the type of cultural capital to be more comfortably involved (Lee & Bowen, 2006), and multiple studies suggest that parental involvement is more predictive of academic success for White and Asian students than it is for Black and Latino students. Furthermore, Black students are subject to disproportionately more disciplinary procedures in school, which can cause them to miss more class time and lead to multiple challenges that influence academic achievement (Davis & Jordan, 1994).

Critical Language Awareness for Social Justice in Education

Given the many other factors associated with student achievement, the inconsistency and methodological shortcomings in language gap research, and the research revealing how linguistic and sociolinguistic differences between homes and schools impact educational opportunity, we argue that ensuring educational equity for culturally and linguistically diverse students begins with an interrogation of linguistic and sociolinguistic hierarchies in which middle-class discursive features and norms are positioned as inherently superior, while others continue to be devalued and marginalized as not only inferior but, in fact, harmful.

Teacher training will be important because, by normalizing language deficit ideologies, language gap discourse may impact teacher attitudes, and research on teacher attitudes reveals a potential Pygmalion effect (Rosenthal & Jacobson, 1992) whereby teacher expectations impact student success. So, if teachers believe that low-income students and/or students who speak a marginalized variety of English are less likely to succeed, this may become a self-fulfilling prophecy. Most future teachers must go through formal university teacher preparation programs and pass strict assessments to earn their teaching credentials. Therefore, pre-service and in-service teacher education needs to focus on understanding linguistic and sociolinguistic diversity and interrogating linguistic and cultural hierarchies, thus incorporating what Alim (2005) calls critical language awareness, which "interrogates the dominating discourse on language and literacy and foregrounds…the examination and interconnectedness of identities, ideologies, histories/herstories, and the hierarchical nature of power relations between groups" (p. 28). Standing on a common platform for viewing language use in relation to broader social dynamics, educators and students can co-construct classroom narratives that: (1) draw attention to raciolinguistic biases and their role in school settings (Flores & Rosa, 2015); (2) honor students' linguistic "funds of knowledge" as valuable tools to promote academic achievement (González et al., 2005); and (3) move beyond a deficit perspective of the communication patterns of low-income families.

It is also worth considering the cultural and linguistic diversity of our teachers – over 80% of teachers in the U.S. come from a White, English-speaking backgrounds (National Center for Education Statistics, 2016), a number that is much higher in most individual states (e.g., 87 percent in Washington State, see Office of Superintendent of Public Instruction, 2018). This contributes to a context where most teachers come from similar (socio)linguistic, academic, and economic backgrounds (Hrabowski & Sanders, 2015; National Center for Education Statistics, 2016). Thus, we need to improve the underrepresentation of students of color and multilingual/multidialectal individuals in university teacher preparation programs to become more representative of the schools in which they will teach. This is not meant to blame educators, however. Pedagogical practices and family engagement patterns are a part of an educational and societal structure that has become entrenched, but is also reproduced, in school systems across the United States and around the world.

The challenge is formidable and seemingly intractable, but the solution must start with a recognition of the diverse cultural and linguistic resources that students bring to school. Initiating such a campaign within schools has the potential to cultivate learning environments that are more educationally conducive for culturally and linguistically diverse students, while simultaneously supporting efforts to transform broader social perspectives towards low-income communities. Focusing on professional development efforts might seem most tangible within contexts like teacher preparation programs, school districts, and state departments of education; however, efforts to resist deficit orientations also require work in community spaces like local libraries, daycare centers, pediatric clinics, and other parent support programs. In concert with these types of grassroots engagement efforts that emphasize linguistic strengths (vs. deficits), there must be clear strategies for engaging school systems and community organizations to provide feasible methods for partnering with linguistically diverse families. These types of partnerships are contextually based, so we endorse outreach efforts that bring together educators, families, linguists, medical professionals, and community organizations to collaboratively map out strategies that best align with the needs of all stakeholders involved. We also encourage promoting such collaborations with the media – something that has been woefully absent in public conversations about the language gap. All of this constitutes an ideological and educational sea change, but nothing less is needed if the goal is true educational equality.

We understand that not everyone will become a teacher, or have immediate access to the educational environment of students from linguistic and cultural backgrounds different from their own. There are multiple other ways to work towards social justice and reject the language gap ideology, including engaging with political leaders, educators, or other community groups. Activist-oriented groups (or individuals) can launch social media campaigns to counter mainstream media stories on the language gap. On an individual level, parents can join their children's parent-teacher organization at school and challenge language deficit biases when necessary. Individuals can volunteer in after-school programs and mentor students from diverse backgrounds to support their academic and personal growth while reinforcing their cultural background as a strength. We also encourage more students and scholars to consider conducting research that both seeks to understand the linguistic skills of minoritized communities and draws attention to other sociopolitical factors that perpetuate academic and economic inequities.

While the language gap appears to focus on improving academic and economic opportunities for people from low-income backgrounds, it is actually a reflection of broader social inequities that have been historically contoured along racial and class divides. In this case, economic status is positioned as the pathology that derails linguistic and cognitive development, which provides a tangible target and method of remediation: poor parents talk to their kids wrong. These types of campaigns to "modify others to be like us" promote bleaching out linguistic diversity by homogenizing communication patterns across all racial, economic, and cultural contexts to reflect White middle- and upper-class language norms. By taking an individual stance against ideologies of linguistic and cultural superiority, everyone can help redirect the conversation away from language diversity as the problem and refocus our attention on the structural issues that continue to anchor systemic inequities and derail educational opportunities for children from linguistically and economically minoritized communities.

References

Alim, H. S. (2005). Critical language awareness in the United States: Revisiting issues and revising pedagogies in a resegregated society. *Educational Researcher*, 34(7), 24–31.

Ashdown, B. K., & Faherty, A. N.(Eds) (2020). *Parents and caregivers across cultures*. Springer.

Avineri, N., Johnson, E. J., Brice-Heath, S., McCarty, T., Ochs, E., Kremer-Sadlik, T., Blum, S., Zentella, A. C., Rosa, J., Flores, N., Alim, H. S., & Paris, D. (2015). Invited forum: Bridging the "language gap." *Journal of Linguistic Anthropology*, 25(1), 66–86.

Avineri, N., Graham, L. R., Johnson, E. J., Riner, R., & Rosa, J. (Eds). (2019). *Language and social justice in practice*. Routledge.

Becker, B. E., & Luthar, S. S. (2002). Social-emotional factors affecting achievement outcomes among disadvantaged students: Closing the achievement gap. *Educational Psychologist*, 37(4), 197–214.

Burchinal, M., McCartney, K., Steinberg, L., Crosnoe, R., Friedman, S. L., McLoyd, V., & Pianta, R. (2011). Examining the black-white achievement gap among low-income children using the NICHD study of early child care and youth development. *Child Development*, 82(5), 1404–1420.

Davis, J. E., & Jordan, W. J. (1994). The effects of school context, structure, and experiences on African American males in middle and high schools. *Journal of Negro Education*, 63, 570–587.

Delpit, L. (2006). *Other people's children: Cultural conflict in the classroom.* The New Press.

Fernald, A., Marchman, V. A., & Weisleder, A. (2013). SES differences in language processing skill and vocabulary are evident at 18 months. *Developmental Science,* 16(2), 234–248.

Flores, N., & Rosa, J. (2015). Undoing appropriateness: Raciolinguistic ideologies and language diversity in education. *Harvard Educational Review,* 85(2), 149–171.

Gay, G. (2010). *Culturally responsive teaching: Theory, research and practice.* Teachers College Press.

Golinkoff, R. M., Hoff, E., Rowe, M. L., & Hirsh-Pasek, K. (2019). Language matters: Denying the existence of the 30-million-word gap has serious consequences. *Child Development,* 90(3), 985–992.

González, N., Moll, L. C., & Amanti, C. (Eds). (2005). *Funds of knowledge: Theorizing practices in households, communities, and classrooms.* Routledge.

Gregory, A., Cornell, D., Fan, X., Sheras, P., Shih, T. H., & Huang, F. (2010). Authoritative school discipline: High school practices associated with lower bullying and victimization. *Journal of Educational Psychology,* 102(2), 483–496.

Hadjistassou, S. K. (2008). Deficit-based education theory. In J. González (Ed.), *Encyclopedia of bilingual education, Vol. 2* (pp. 218–222). Sage.

Hart, B., & Risley, T. R. (1992). American parenting of language-learning children: Persisting differences in family-child interactions observed in natural home environments. *Developmental Psychology,* 28(6), 1096–1105.

Hart, B., & Risley, T. (1995). *Meaningful differences in the everyday experiences of young American children.* Brookes Publishing.

Heath, S. B. (1983). *Ways with words: Language, life and work in communities and classrooms.* Cambridge University Press.

Heath, S. B. (2000). Linguistics in the study of language in education. *Harvard Educational Review,* 70(1), 49–59.

Hirsh-Pasek, K., Adamson, L. B., Bakeman, R., Owen, M. T., Golinkoff, R. M., Pace, A., Yust, P. K. S, & Suma, K. (2015). The contribution of early communication quality to low-income children's language success. *Psychological Science,* 26 (7), 1071–1083.

Hoff, E. (2013). Interpreting the early language trajectories of children from low-SES and language minority homes: implications for closing achievement gaps. *Developmental Psychology,* 49(1), 4–14.

Hrabowski, F. A., & Sanders, M. G. (2015). Increasing racial diversity in the teacher workforce: One university's approach. *NEA Higher Education Journal: Thought & Action,* Winter, 101–116.

Rosenthal, R., & Jacobson, L. (1992). *Pygmalion in the classroom: Teacher expectation and pupils' intellectual development.* Irvington Publishers.

Johnson, D. C., & Johnson, E. J. (2015). Power and agency in language policy appropriation. *Language Policy,* 14(3), 221–243.

Kozol, J. (1991). *Savage inequalities: Children in America's schools.* Crown Publishing Group.

Kurkul, K., & Corriveau, K. (2017). Question, explanation, follow-up: A mechanism for learning from others? *Child Development,* 89(1), 280–294.

Labov, W. (1972). *Language in the inner city: Studies in the black English vernacular.* University of Pennsylvania Press.

Ladson-Billings, G. (1995). Toward a theory of culturally relevant pedagogy. *American Educational Research Journal,* 32(3), 465–491.

Ladson-Billings, G. (2014). Culturally relevant pedagogy 2.0: a.k.a the remix. *Harvard Educational Review*, 84(1), 74–84.

Ladson-Billings, G. (2017). "Makes me wanna holler": Refuting the "culture of poverty" discourse in urban schooling. *American Academy of Political and Social Science*, 673, 80–90.

Lee, J. S., & Bowen, N. K. (2006). Parent involvement, cultural capital, and the achievement gap among elementary school children. *American Educational Research Journal*, 43(2), 193–218.

Leffel, K., & Suskind, D. (2013). Parent-directed approaches to enrich the early language environments of children living in poverty. *Seminars in Speech and Language*, 34(4), 267–277.

McCarty, T. L. (Ed.). (2005). *Language, literacy, and power in schooling*. Lawrence Erlbaum Associates.

National Center for Education Statistics. (2016). The state of racial diversity in the educator workforce. https://nces.ed.gov/programs/digest/d13/tables/dt13_209.10.asp

Neuman, S. B. (2006). The knowledge gap: Implications for early education. In D. K. Dickinson & S. B. Neuman (Eds), *Handbook of early literacy research, Vol. 2* (pp. 29–40). Guilford Press.

Ochs, E., & Schieffelin, B. (2014). The theory of language socialization. In A. Druanti, E. Ochs, & B. B. Schieffelin (Eds), *The handbook of language socialization* (pp. 1–22). Wiley Blackwell.

Office of Superintendent of Public Instruction. (2018). Classroom teachers by teacher demographics (2017–2018). https://washingtonstatereportcard.ospi.k12.wa.us/ReportCard/ViewSchoolOrDistrict/103300

Paris, D., & Alim, H. S. (2014). What are we seeking to sustain through culturally sustaining pedagogy? A loving critique forward. *Harvard Educational Review*, 84(1), 85–100.

Paris, D., & Alim, S. H. (Eds). (2017). *Culturally sustaining pedagogies: Teaching and learning for justice in a changing world*. Teachers College Press.

Philips, S. U. (1983). *The invisible culture: Communication in classroom and community on the Warm Springs Reservation*. Waveland Press.

Rolstad, K. (2014). Rethinking language at school. *International Multilingual Research Journal*, 8(1), 1–8.

Rowe, M. L. (2008). Child-directed speech: Relation to socioeconomic status, knowledge of child development and child vocabulary skill. *Journal of Child Language*, 35 (1), 185–205.

Rowe, M. L. (2012). A longitudinal investigation of the role of quantity and quality of child-directed speech in vocabulary development. *Child Development*, 83(5), 1762–1774.

Ruiz, R. (1990). Official languages and language planning. In K. L. Adams & D. T. Brink (Eds), *Perspectives on official English: The campaign for English as the official language of the USA* (pp. 11–24). Mouton de Gruyter.

Snow, C. E. (2017). The role of vocabulary versus knowledge in children's language learning: A fifty-year perspective. *Infancia y Aprendizaje*, 40(1), 1–18.

Spera, C. (2005). A review of the relationship among parenting practices, parenting styles, and adolescent school achievement. *Educational Psychology Review*, 17(2): 125–146.

Suskind, D., Leffel, K. R., Hernandez, M. W., Sapolich, S. G., Suskind, E., Kirkham, E., & Meehan, P. (2013). An exploratory of 'quantitative linguistic feedback': Effect of LENA feedback on adult language production. *Communication Disorders Quarterly*, 34(4), 199–209.

Wasik, B. A., & Hindman, A. H. (2015). Talk alone won't close the 30-million word gap. *Kappan Magazine*, 96(6), 50–54.

Zentella, A.C. (2005). Premises, promises, and pitfalls of language socialization research in Latino families and communities. In A. C. Zentella (Ed.), *Building on strength: Language and literacy in Latino families and communities* (pp. 13–30). Teachers College Press.

INDEX

Note: Page locators in bold refer to tables; those in italics to figures.